Dunnville Ontario Book 2 and Other Haldimand County towns in Colour Photos, Saving Our History One Photo at a Time

Photography
by Barbara Raué
©2018

Series Name: Cruising Ontario

Book 215: Haldimand County Towns

Cover photo: 1575 Highway 3, Dunnville, Page 25

©All the photos in this book have been taken with my cameras. I own the rights to them.

Series Name: Cruising Ontario
Saving Our History One Photo at a Time
in colour photos

Books Available in Alphabetical Order:
Aberfoyle, Acton, Ajax, Alton, Amherstburg, Ancaster, Arthur, Auburn, Aylmer, Ayr, Beaver Valley, Belgrave, Belleville, Bloomingdale, Blyth, Brantford, Brockville, Burford, Burlington, Caledon, Caledonia, Cambridge, Carlow, Chatsworth, Clifford, Collingwood, Conestogo, Delhi, Dorchester to Aylmer, Drayton, Drumbo, Dundas, Dunlop, Eden Mills, Elmira, Elora, Erin, Essex, Fergus, Goderich, Grimsby, Guelph, Hagersville, Hamilton, Hanover, Harriston, Hespeler, Jarvis, Kingston, Kingsville, Kitchener, Lake Superior, Lincoln, Linwood, Listowel, London, Lucknow, Merrickville, Mono, Mount Forest, Mount Pleasant, Neustadt, New Hamburg, Newboro, Newport, Niagara-on-the-Lake, Niagara Falls, North Bay, Oakville, Onondaga, Orangeville, Orillia, Oshawa, Owen Sound, Palmerston, Paris, Pelham, Perth, Peterborough, Petrolia, Pickering, Port Colborne, Port Elgin, Portland, Preston, Rockwood, Sarnia, Sault Ste. Marie, Seaforth, Sheffield, Shelburne, Simcoe, Smiths Falls, Smithville, Southampton, St. Catharines, St. George, St. Jacobs, St. Marys, St. Thomas, Stoney Creek, Stratford, Thamesford, Thunder Bay, Tillsonburg, Toronto, Waterdown, Waterford, Waterloo, Welland, Wellesley, West Flamborough, Westport, Whitby, Windsor, Wingham, Woodstock

Book 210: North Bay
Book 211: Fort Erie
Book 212-215: Haldimand
    County

Table of Contents

Dunnville	Page 5
South Cayuga	Page 28
Sweet's Corners	Page 33
Lakeshore Road	Page 40
Kohler	Page 46
Knight's Beach – Lake Erie	Page 49
Hagersville	Page
Jarvis	Page 50

Haldimand County is a municipality on the Niagara Peninsula in Southern Ontario, on the north shore of Lake Erie, and on the Grand River. Haldimand was first created as a county in 1800, from a portion of Norfolk. It was named after the governor of the Province of Quebec Sir Frederick Haldimand. From 1974 to 2000, Haldimand County and Norfolk County were merged to form the Regional Municipality of Haldimand-Norfolk.

The population centers in Haldimand are Caledonia, Dunnville, Hagersville, Jarvis and Cayuga. Most of Haldimand is agricultural land, although some heavy industry, including the Nanticoke Generating Station, is located here. Some of the smaller communities within the municipality are Byng, Canborough, Canfield, Cheapside, Fisherville, Kohler, Lowbanks, Nanticoke, Rainham Centre, Selkirk, South Cayuga, Sweets Corners, and York.

Dunnville is a community near the mouth of Grand River in Haldimand County, and is only a few kilometers from Lake Erie. Dunnville was one of the early thriving centers of Upper Canada and Ontario. Following the American Revolution, a six mile strip of land on both sides of the Grand River from its mouth to its sources was opened up to settlement by displaced members of the Six Nations Confederacy. The land was granted to the Iroquois tribes by the British to compensate the Confederacy for land lost in the United States during the revolution. The British originally intended the land to remain in the hands of the Indians, but Mohawk Chief Joseph Brant wanted to open it up to settlement in order to create a source of revenue. Brant persuaded the Six Nations to surrender large blocks of land. Many of the early European arrivals were United Empire Loyalists.

South Cayuga lies on the north shore of Lake Erie, ten kilometers east of Dunnville. Initially part of the Six Nations of the Grand River Indian Reserve, the heavy clay soil of South Cayuga Township was well suited to the cultivation of grain, hay, and livestock.

Sweet's Corners is located on Rainham Road west of South Cayuga.

Kohler was named for the Kohler family, one of many German immigrants who came to the area in the mid-1800s. It is located on County Road 8 south of Cayuga, and north of Rainham Centre.

Jarvis is located near the towns of Simcoe, Cayuga, Port Dover and Hagersville. Jarvis is strategically located at the junction of Highways 3 and 6. Jarvis has some excellent examples of brick architecture. Many of the historic homes were built after 1873. Many of the town's restaurants and shops are clustered around the intersection of the highways. The majority of the buildings are red brick.

Dunnville

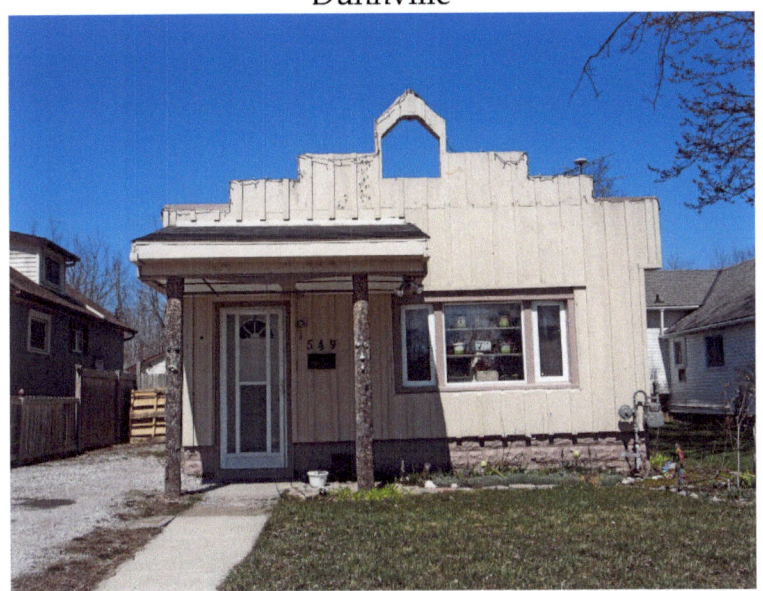

549 Alder Street

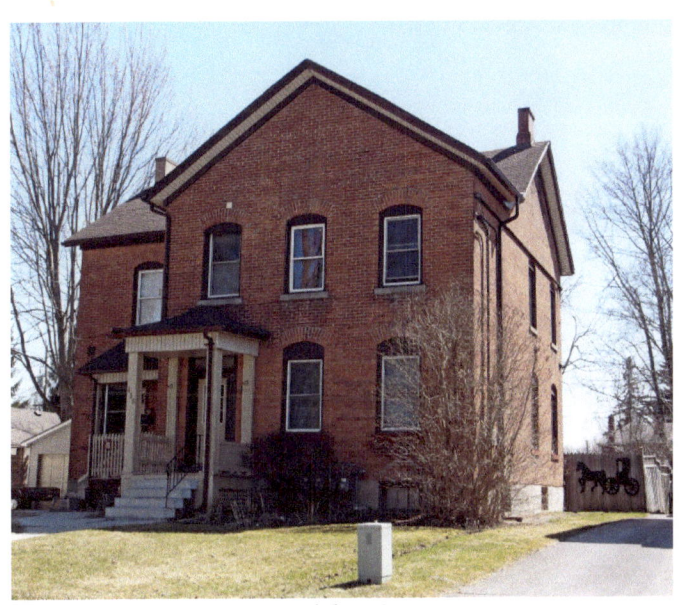

436 Alder Street

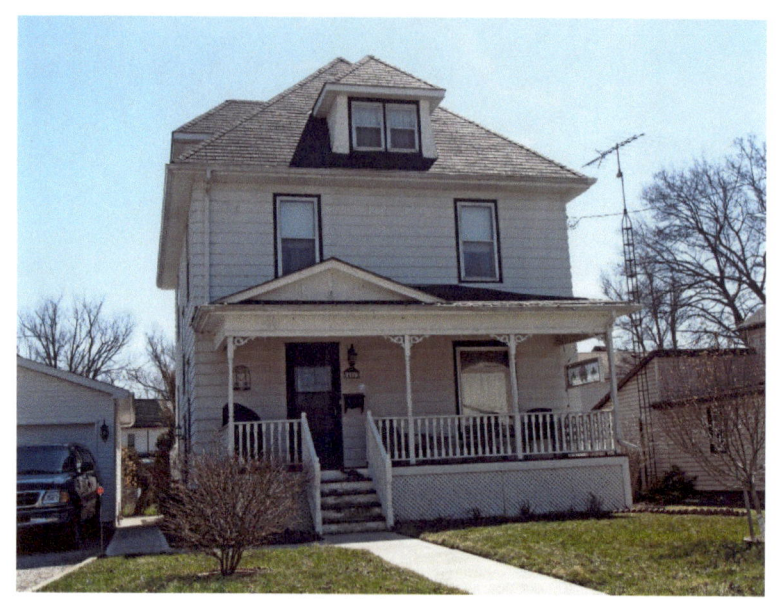

408 Alder Street

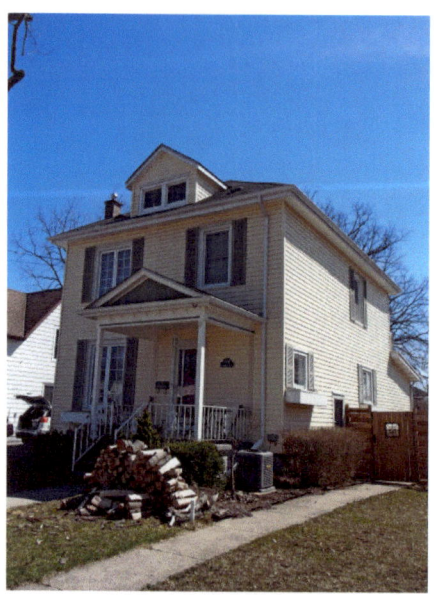

308 Alder Street

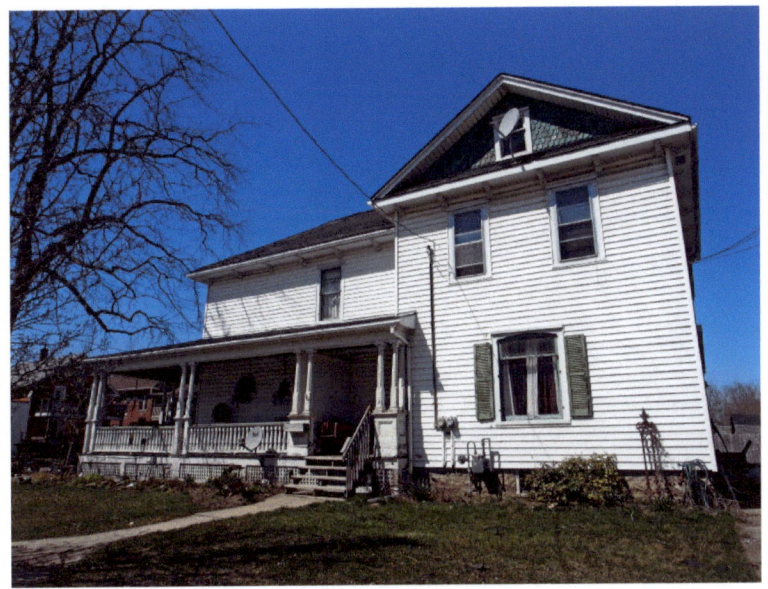

301 Alder Street

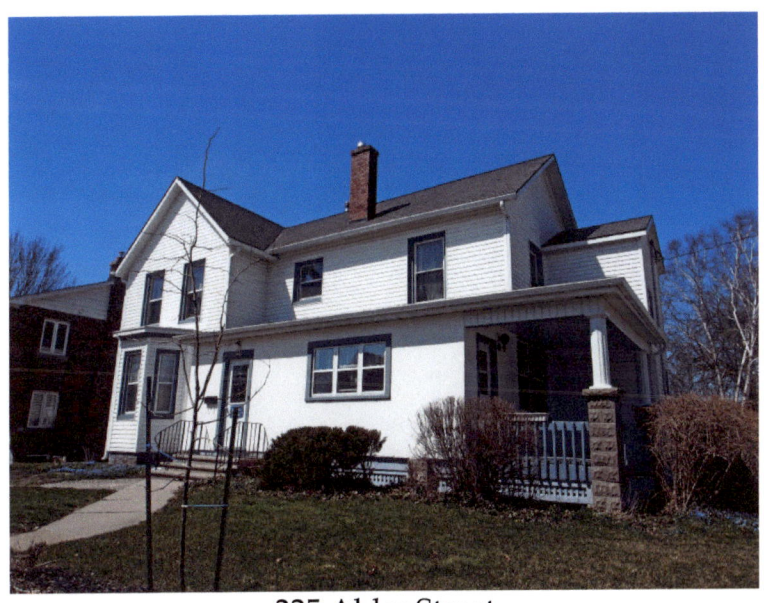

225 Alder Street

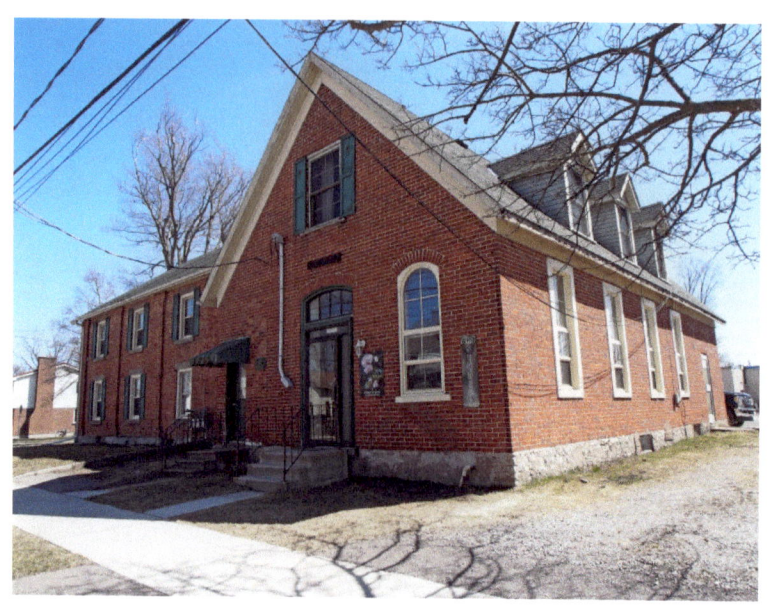

224 Alder Street

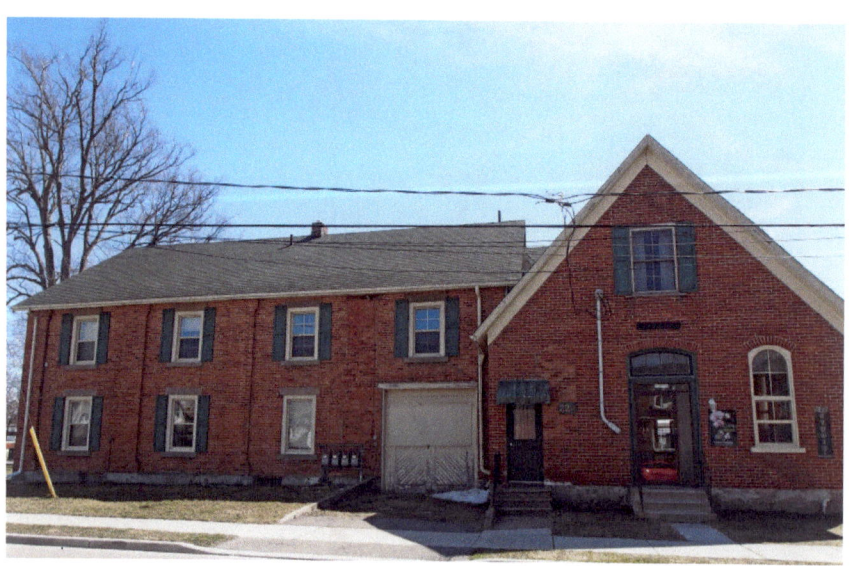

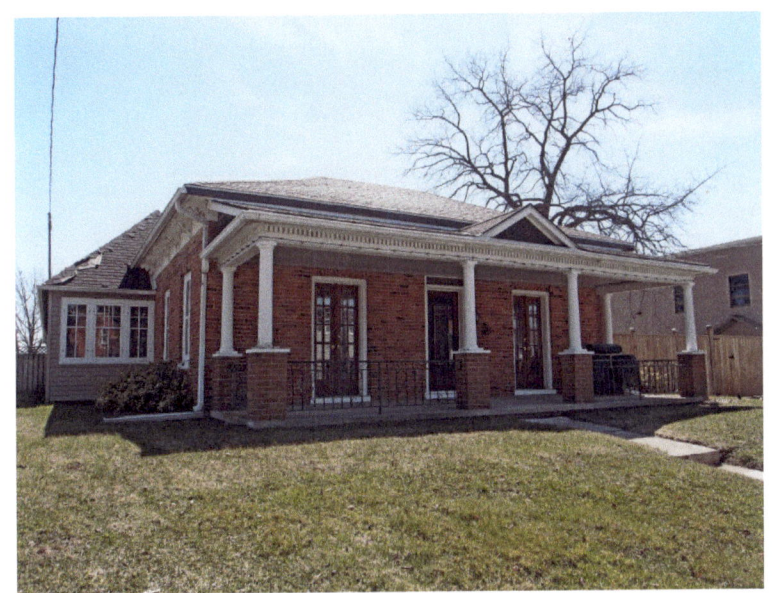

212 Alder Street

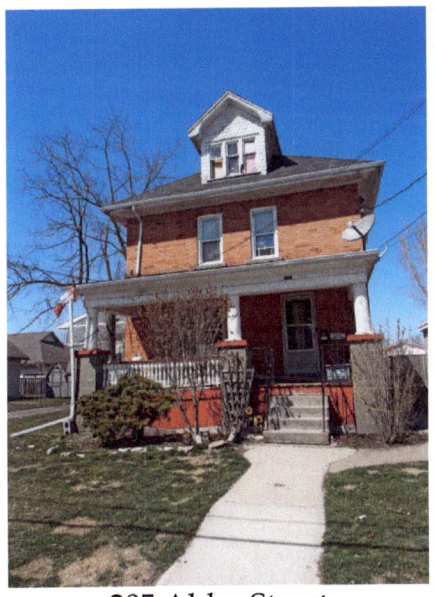

205 Alder Street

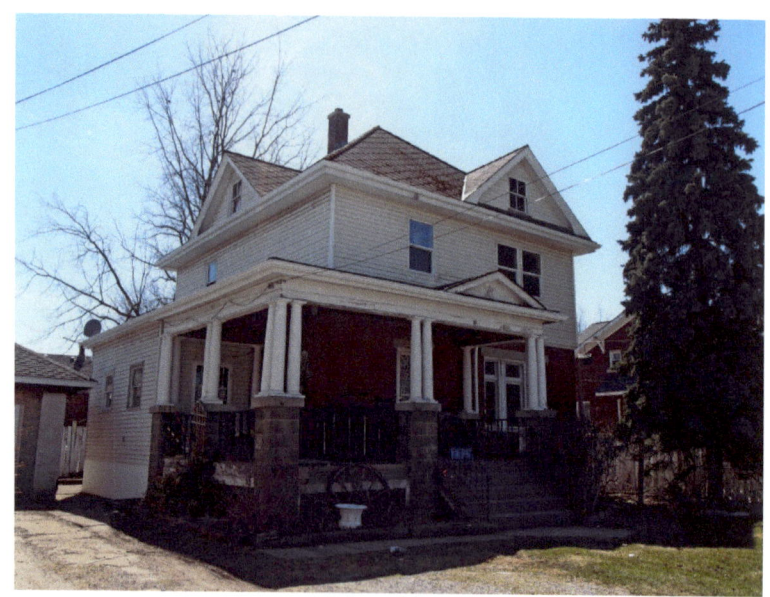

Alder Street

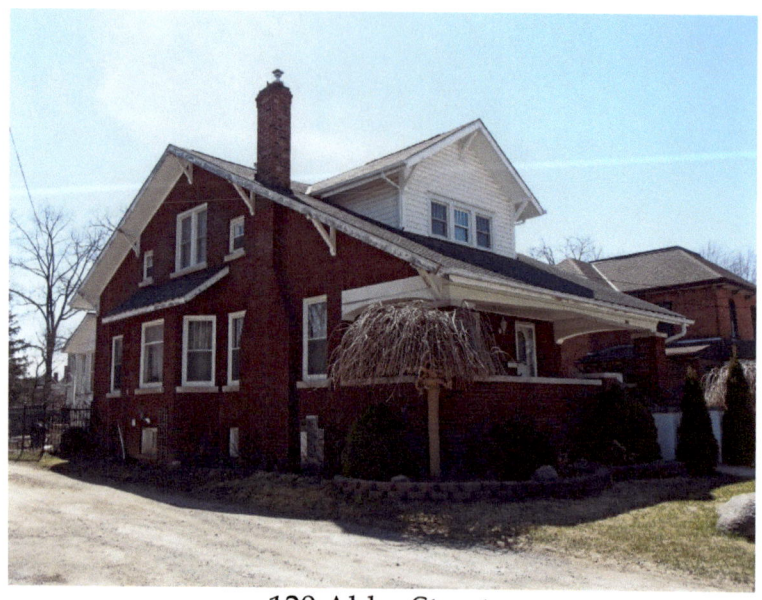

120 Alder Street

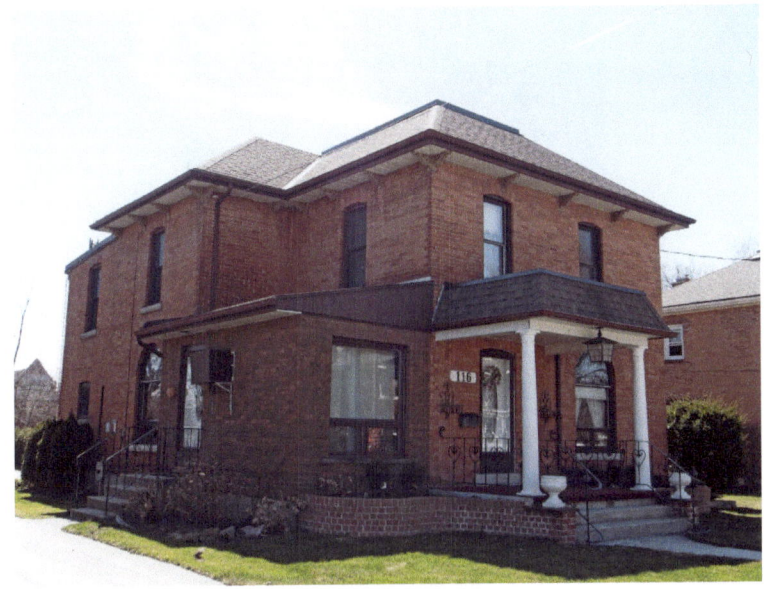

116 Alder Street

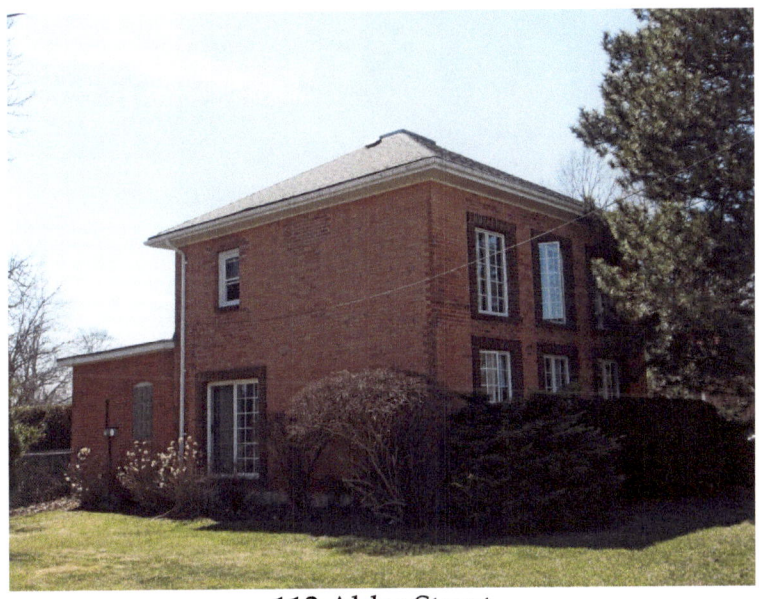

112 Alder Street

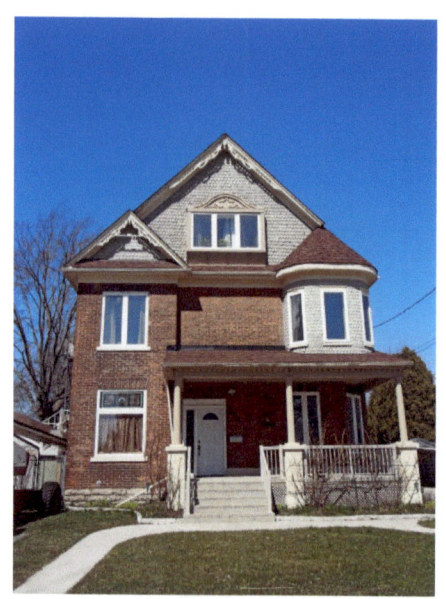

111 Alder Street

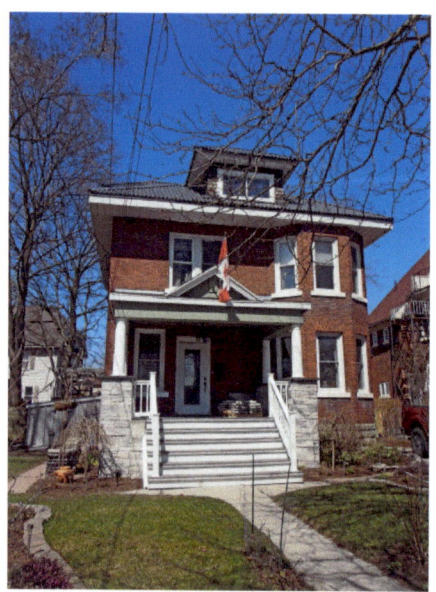

109 Alder Street

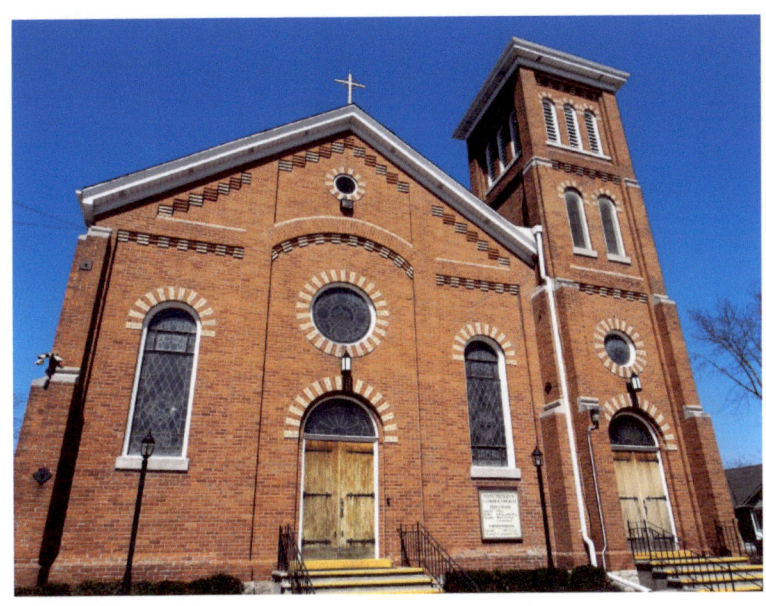

204 Alder Street – Saint Michael's Catholic Church - A.D. 1886

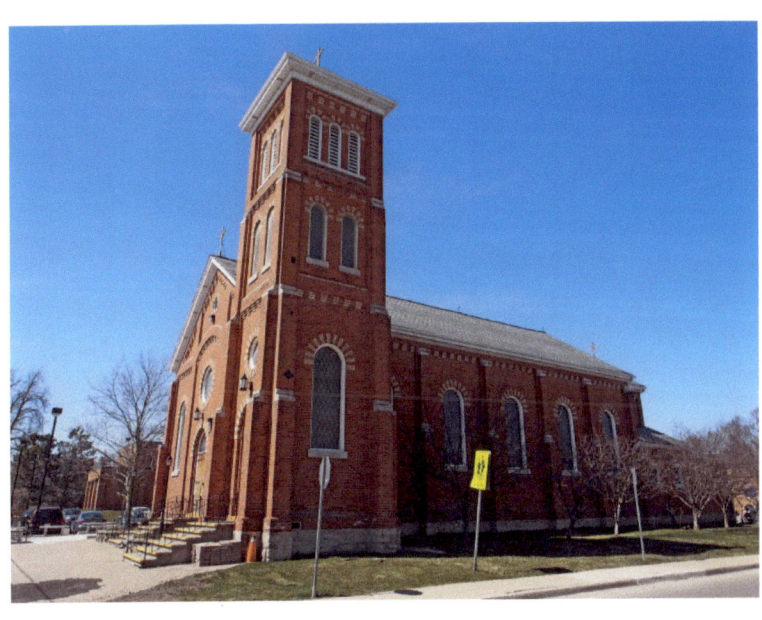

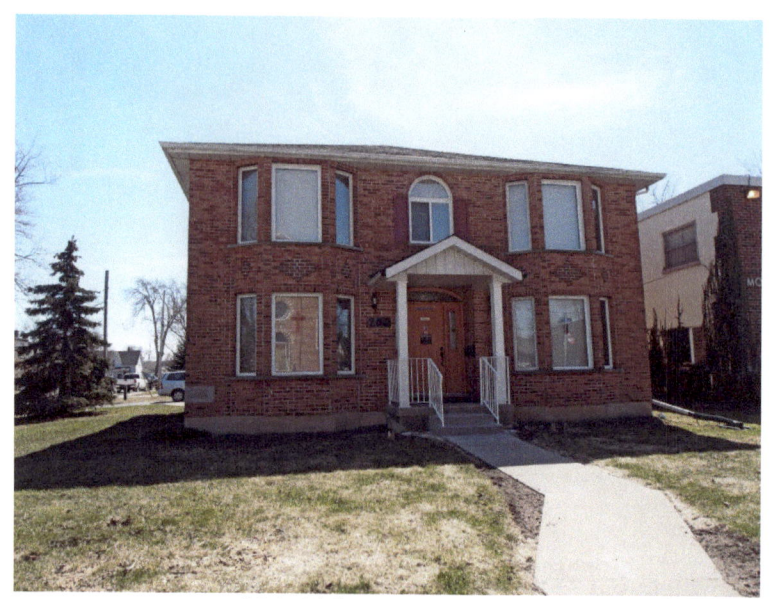

204 Alder Street West

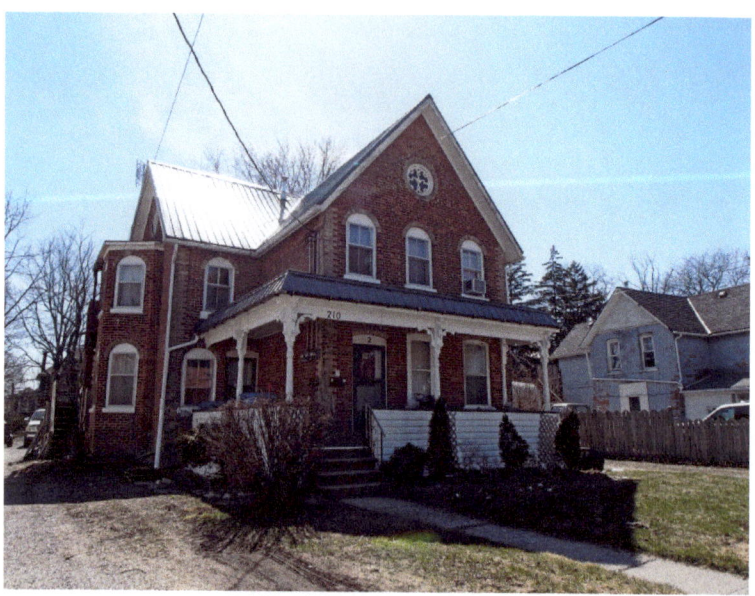

210 Alder Street West

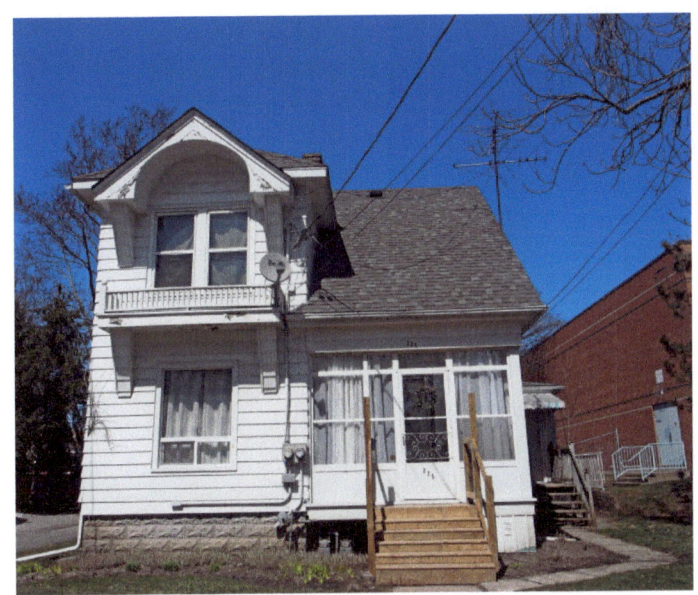

225 Alder Street West

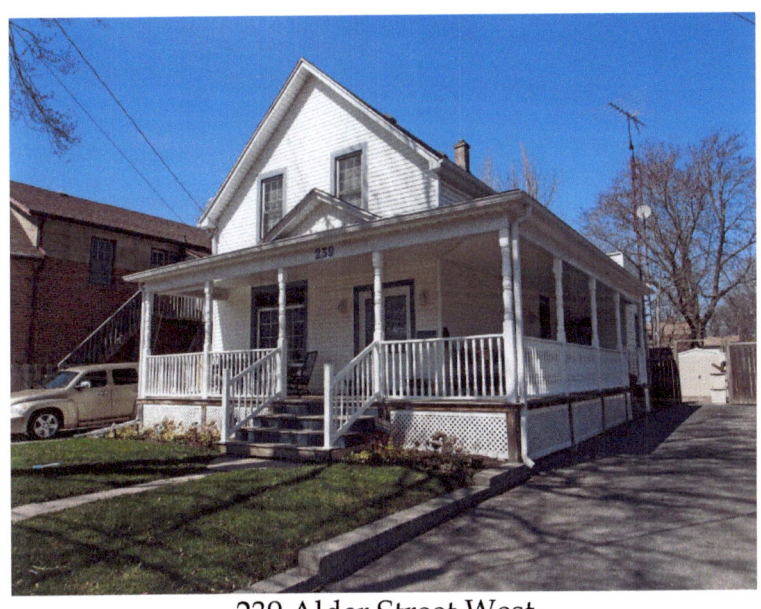

239 Alder Street West

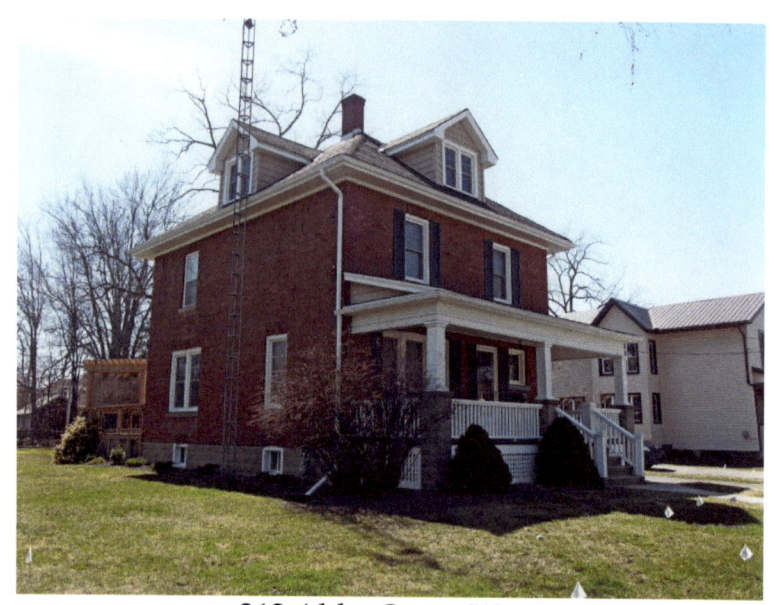
312 Alder Street West

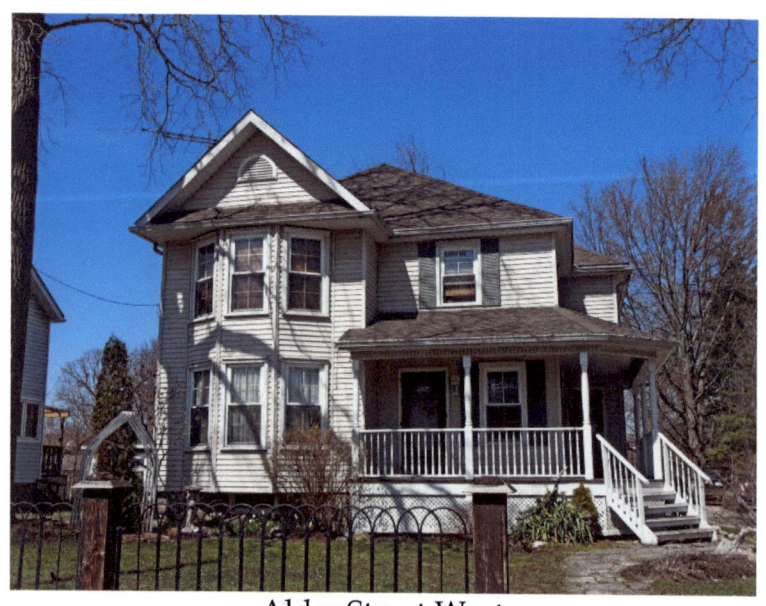
Alder Street West

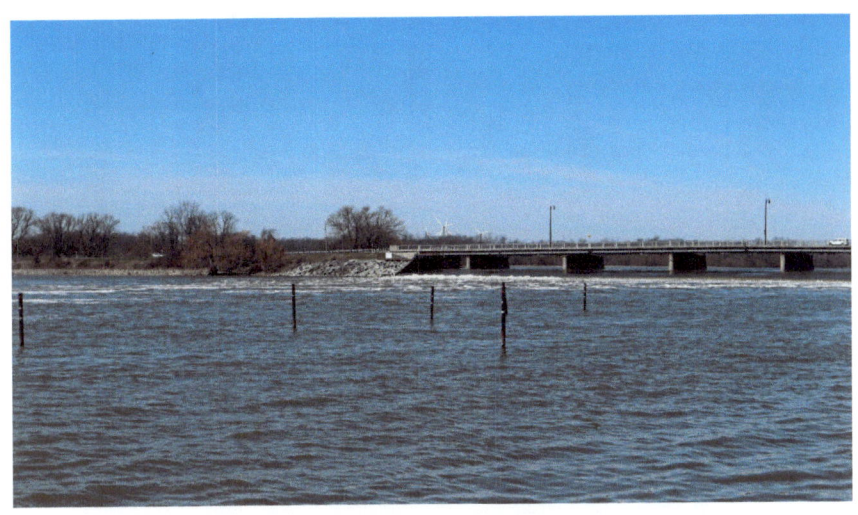

Grand River

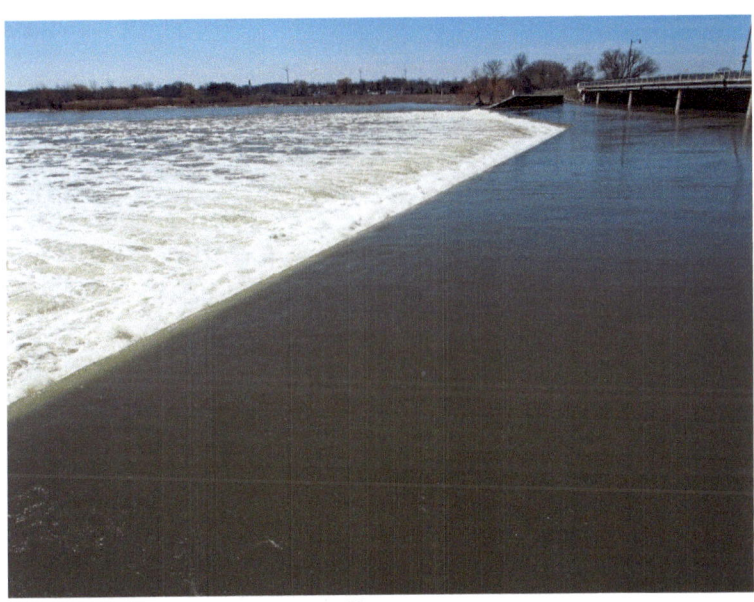

Dam

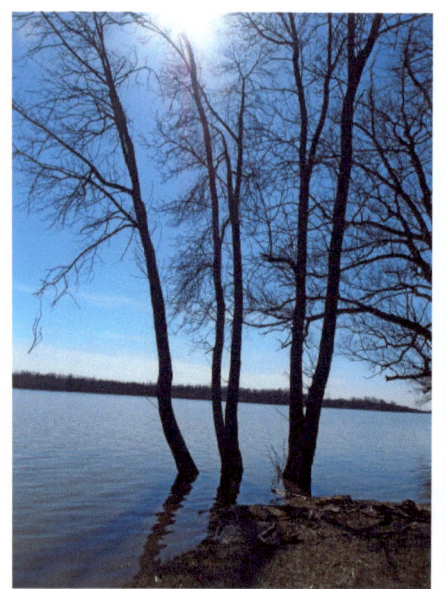 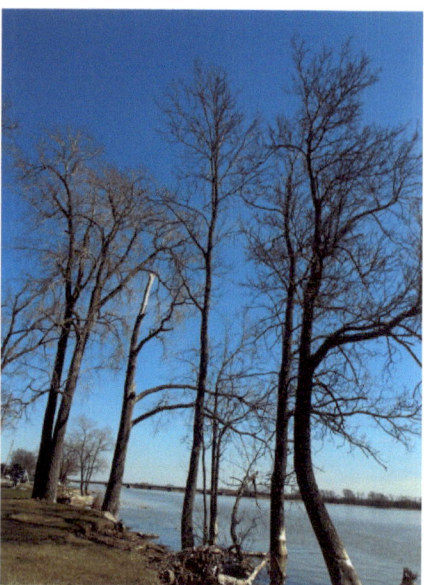

Trees in the edge of the Grand River

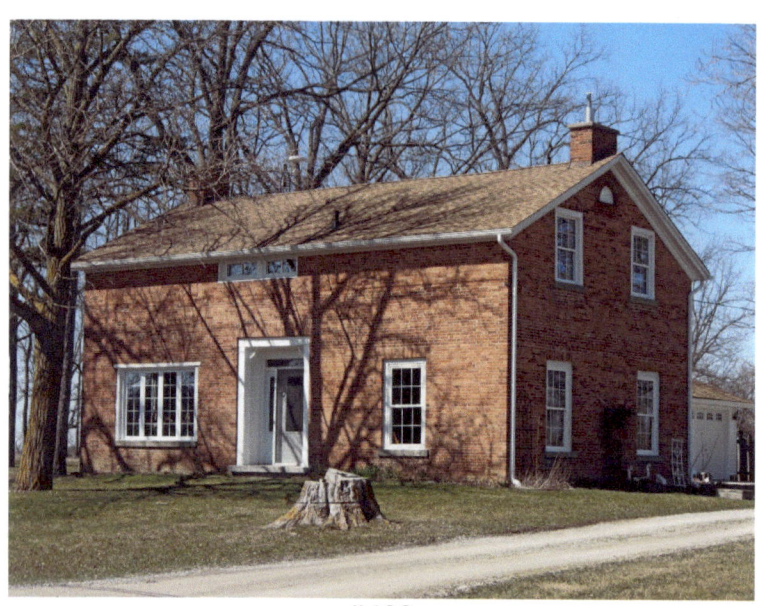

#408

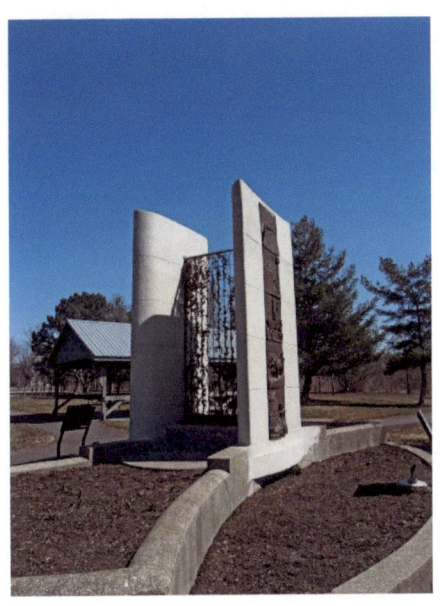

Dunnville Centennial Park Fountain – 1967

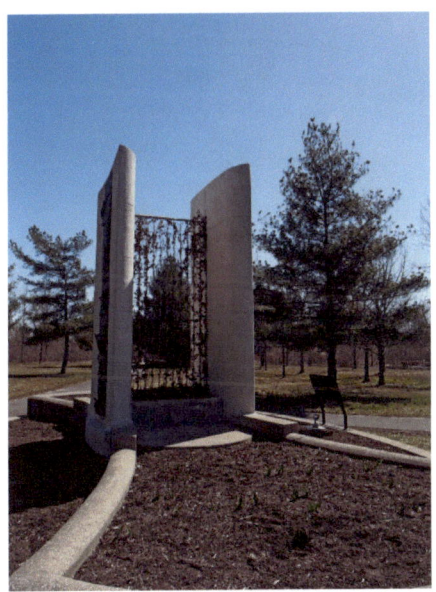

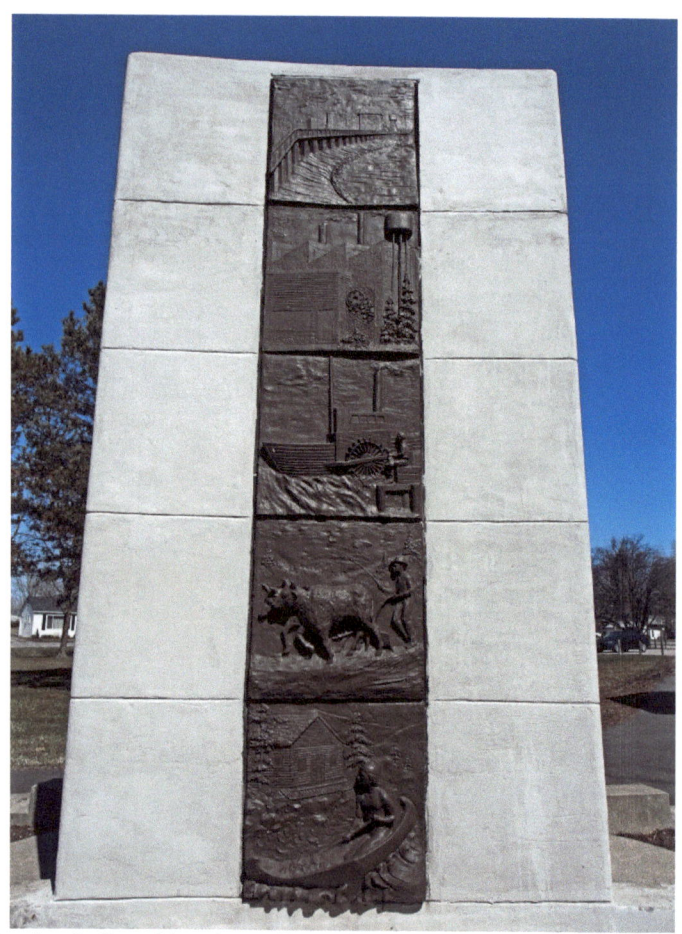

Dr. Elizabeth Bradford Holbrook sculpted the historical panels which line each side of the fountain. These panels depict Dunnville's history and development as a diverse and vibrant community. The bottom panel represents the First Nations settlement; the second panel the advent of European farmers establishing the community's agricultural roots; the center panel celebrates the importance of the Grand River as a heritage waterway with links to the Welland Canal; the fourth panel shows the many mills which spurred Dunnville's growth; and the top panel recognizes Dunnville's iconic dam and bridge.

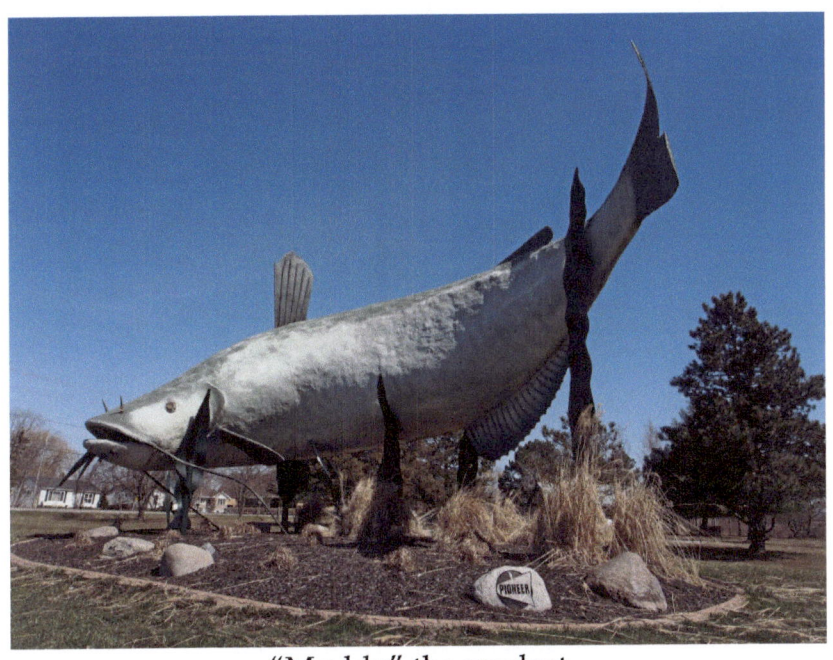

"Muddy" the mudcat
A mudcat is a form of channel catfish and has long been associated with Dunnville. At over fifty feet in length, this is the largest statue of its kind in the world.

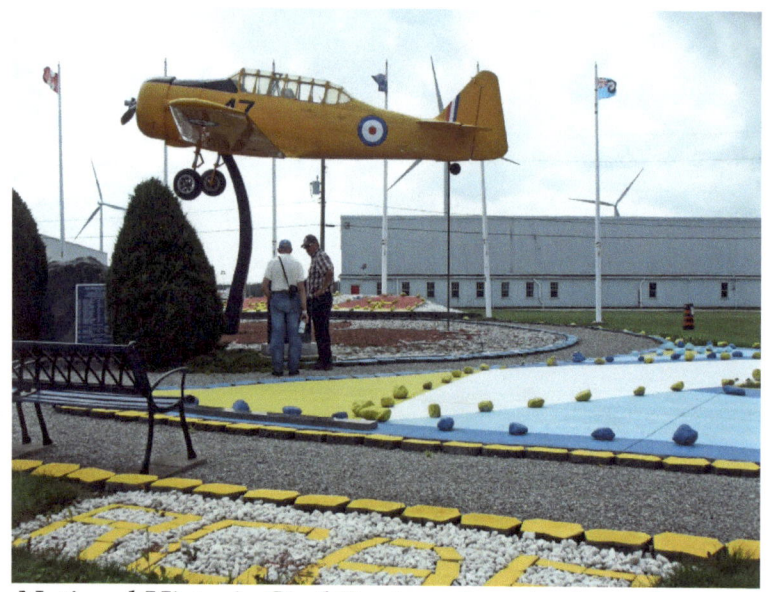

National Historic Civil Engineering site is a tribute to Canada's civil engineers who, between 1940 and 1943, designed and constructed 88 airfields and 88 relief fields together with the infrastructure. The airfields were required by the British Commonwealth Air Training plan which trained more than 250,000 personnel, of whom 131,000 were aircrew, for the allied war effort. This field, Dunnville Airport, was the site of No. 6 Service Flying Training School.

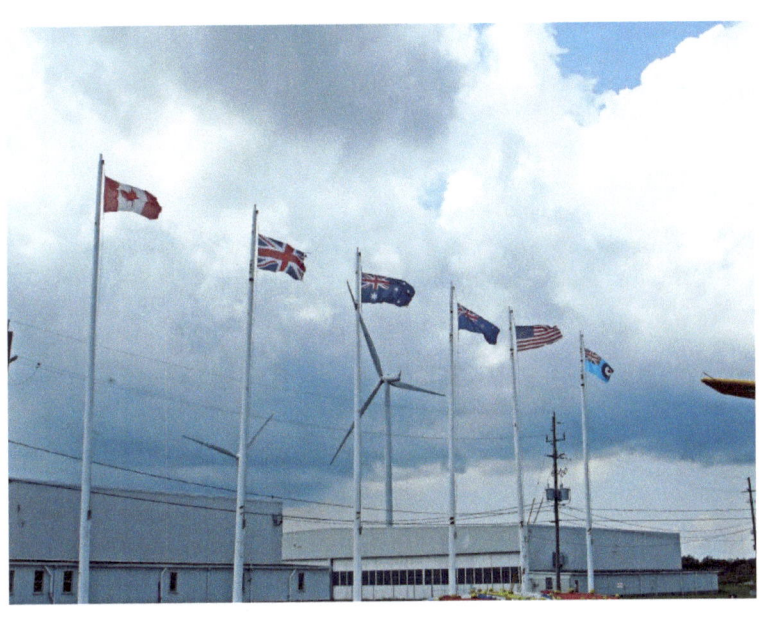

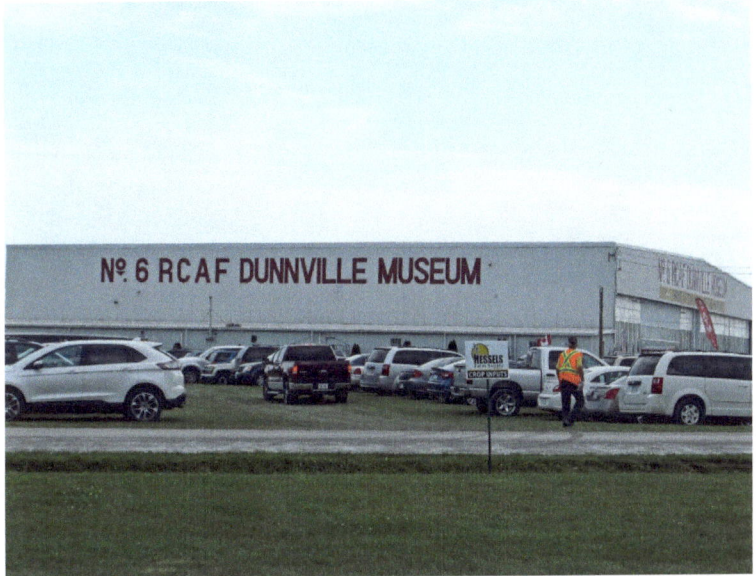

536 Port Maitland Road – Dunnville Museum

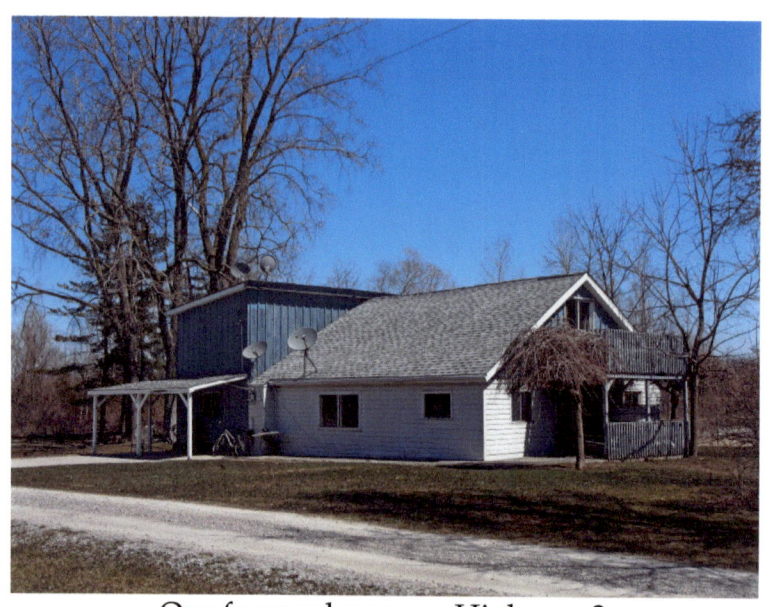
Our former home on Highway 3

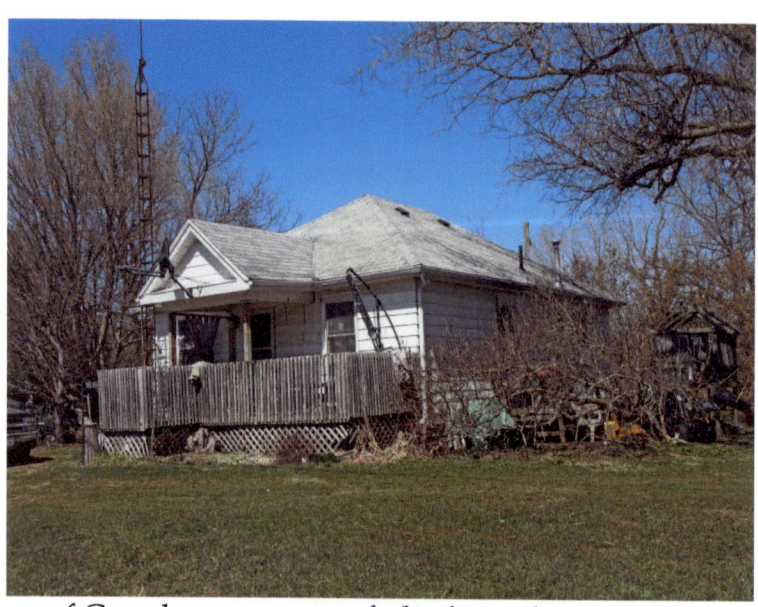
Home of Grandma – my step-father's mother – on Highway 3 in front of our house

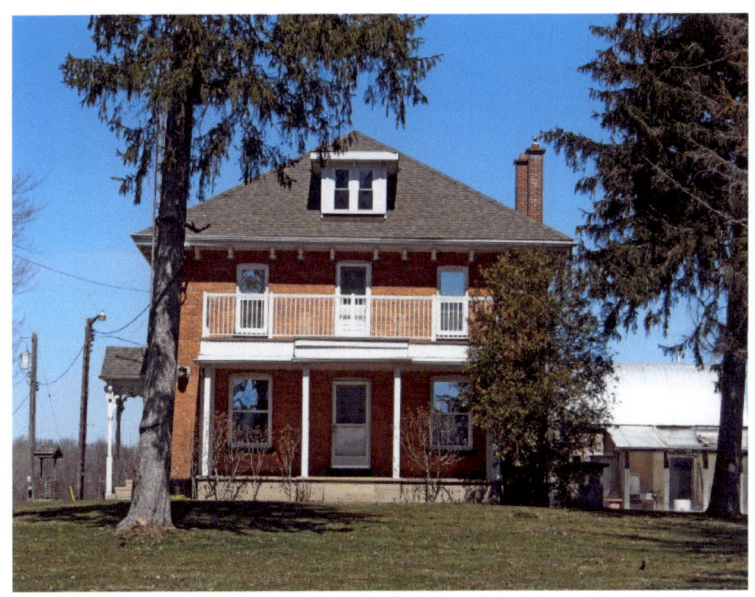

1575 Highway 3

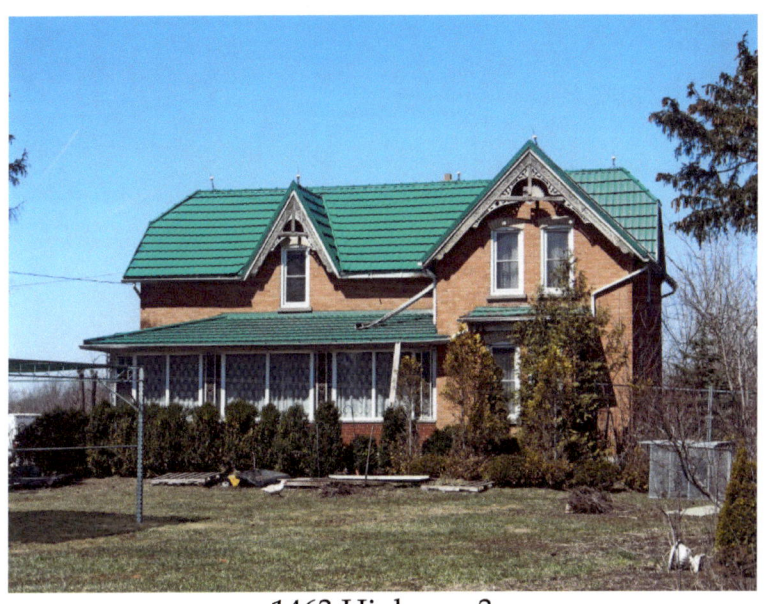

1463 Highway 3

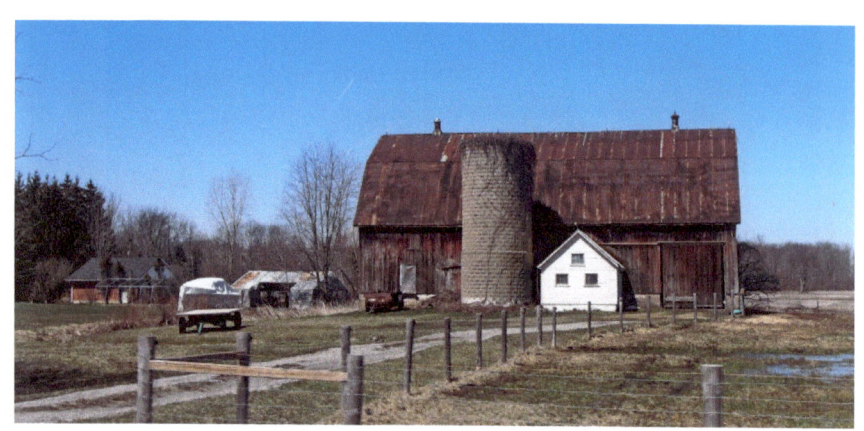

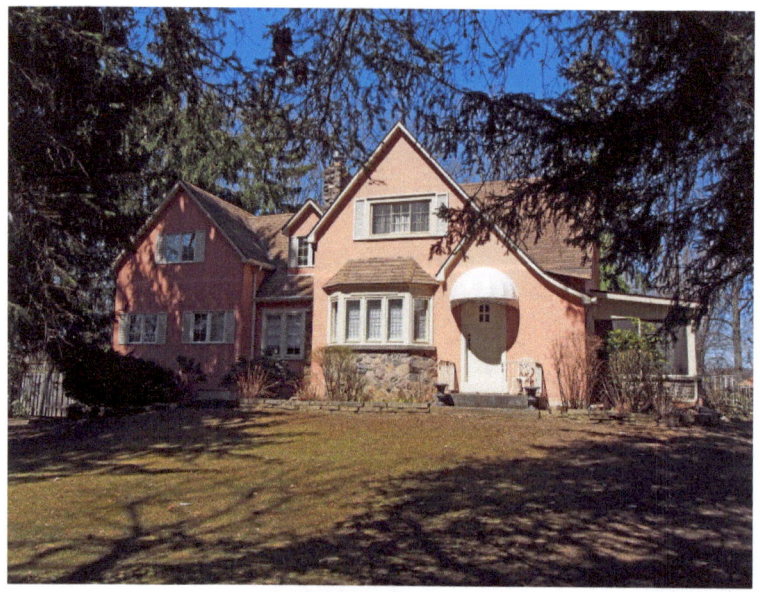

1427 Highway 3

South Cayuga

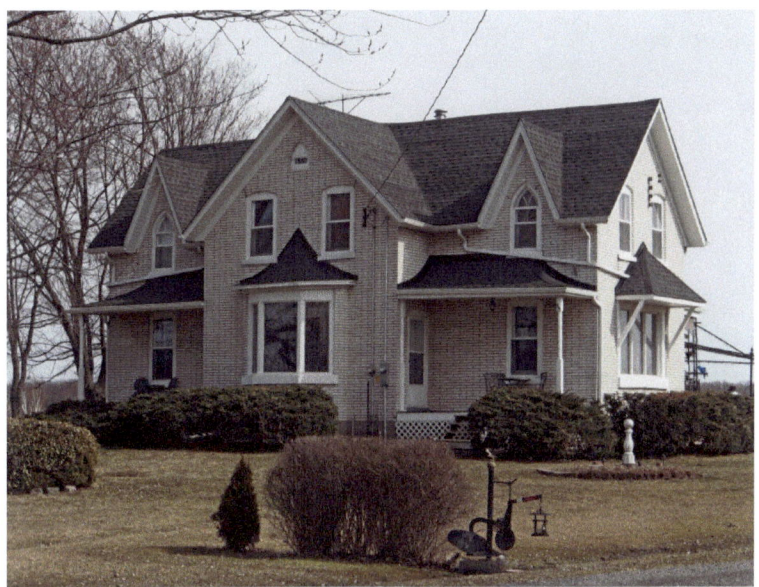

6156 Rainham Road

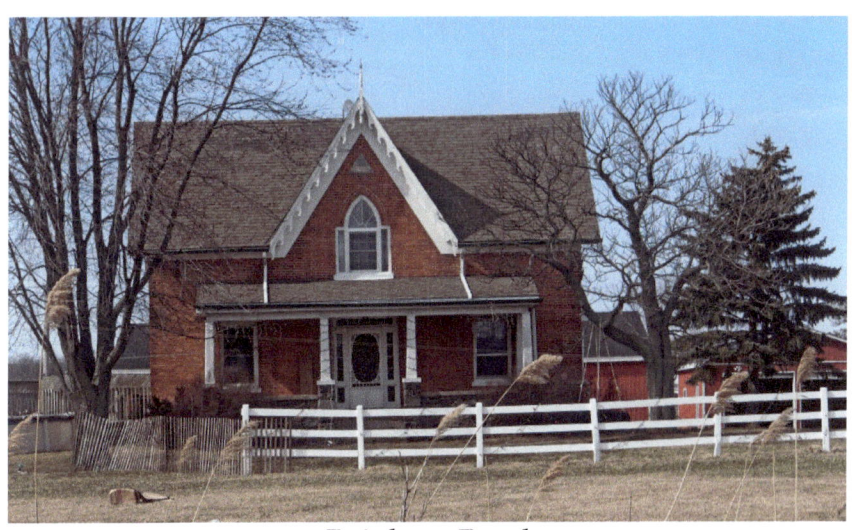

Rainham Road

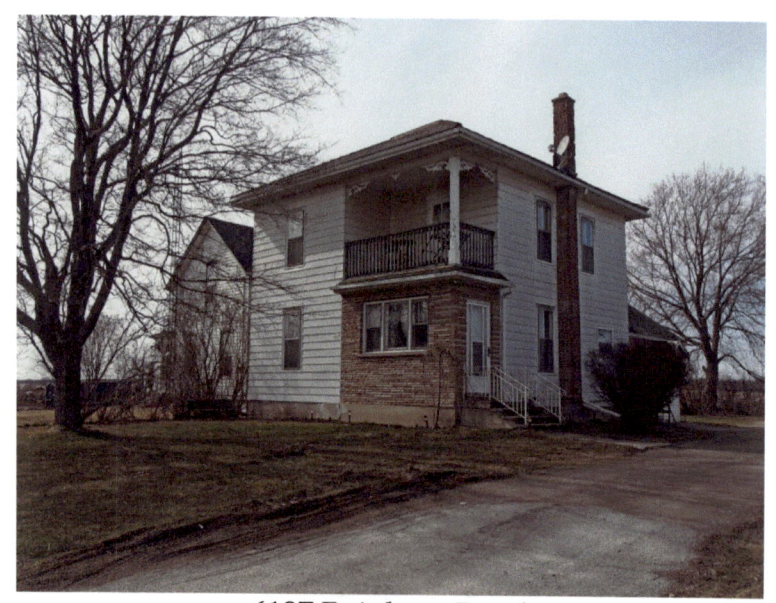

6197 Rainham Road

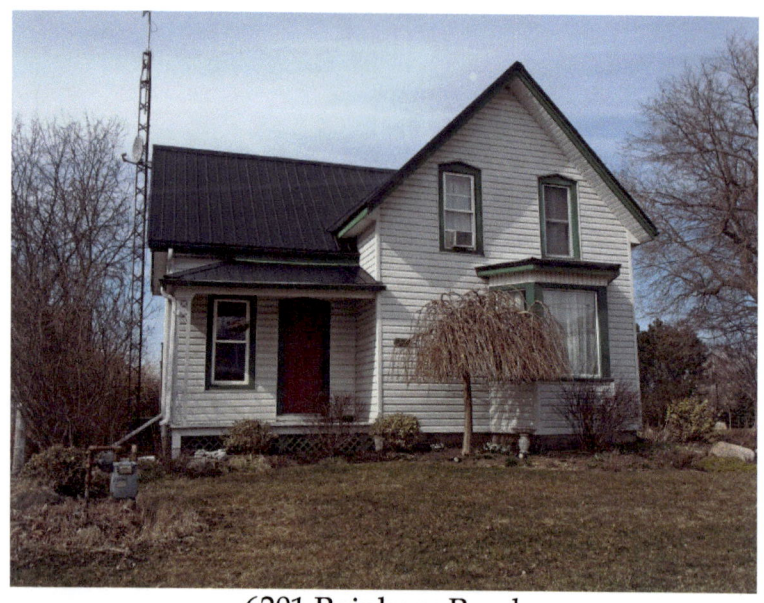

6201 Rainham Road

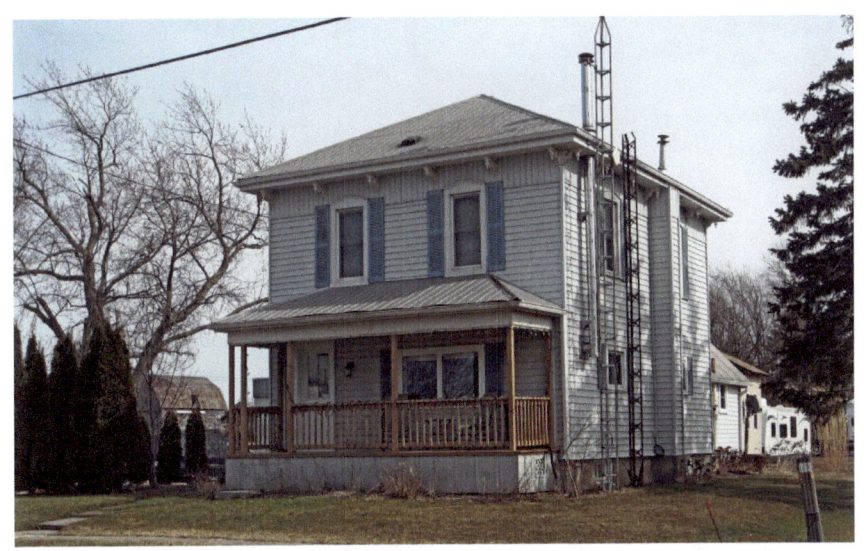
Rainham Road

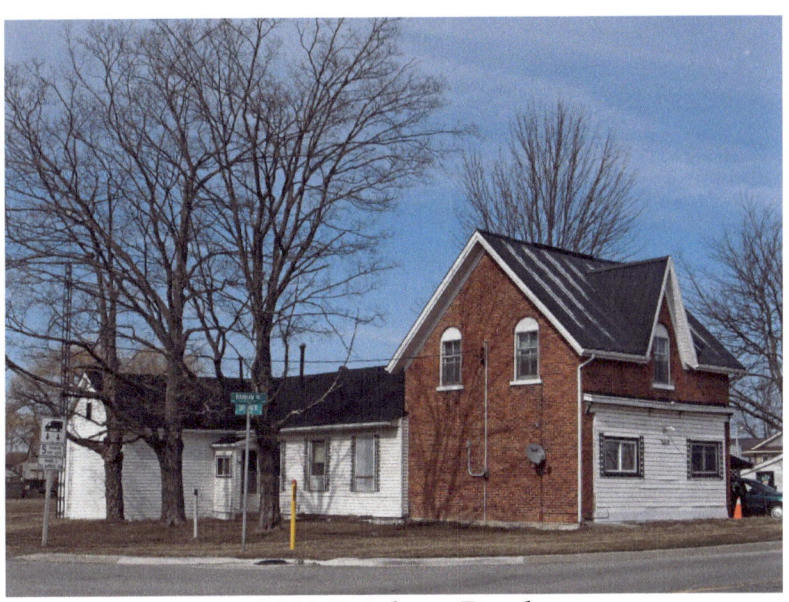
5219 Rainham Road

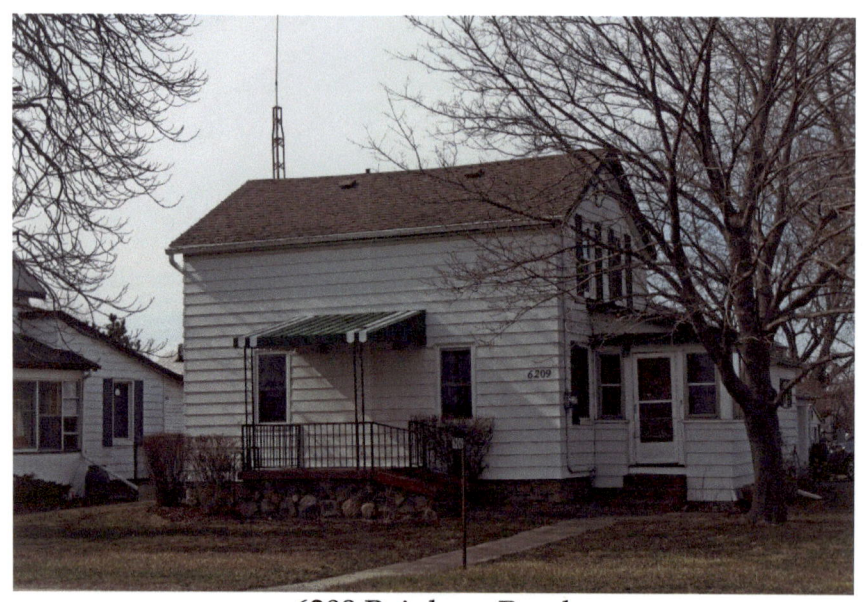

6209 Rainham Road

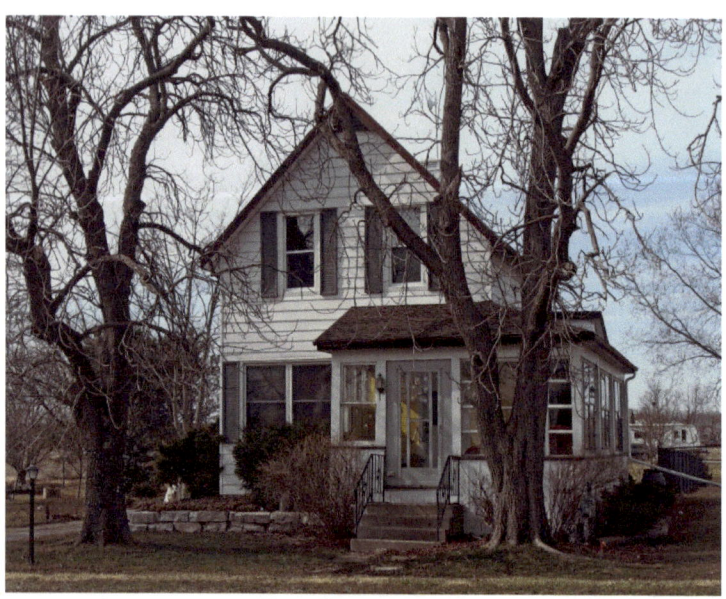

Rainham Road

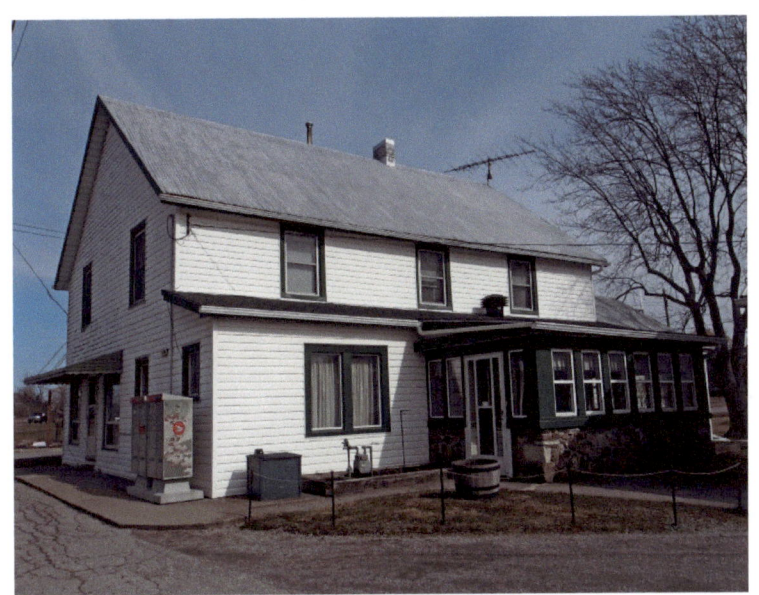

6210 Rainham Road

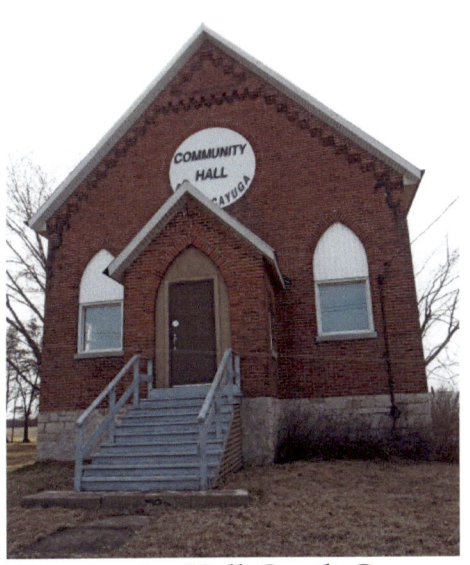

Community Hall, South Cayuga

Sweet's Corners

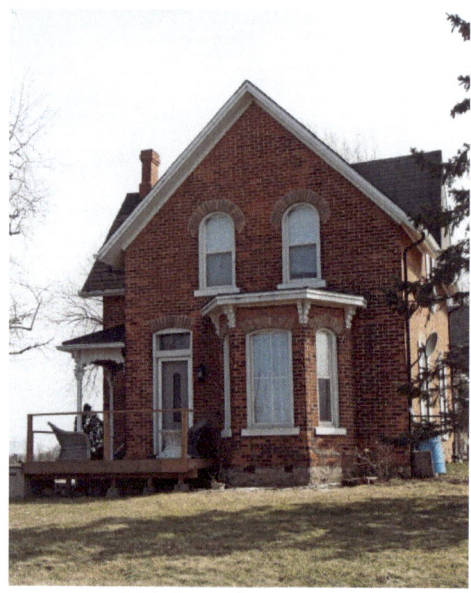

5330 Rainham Road

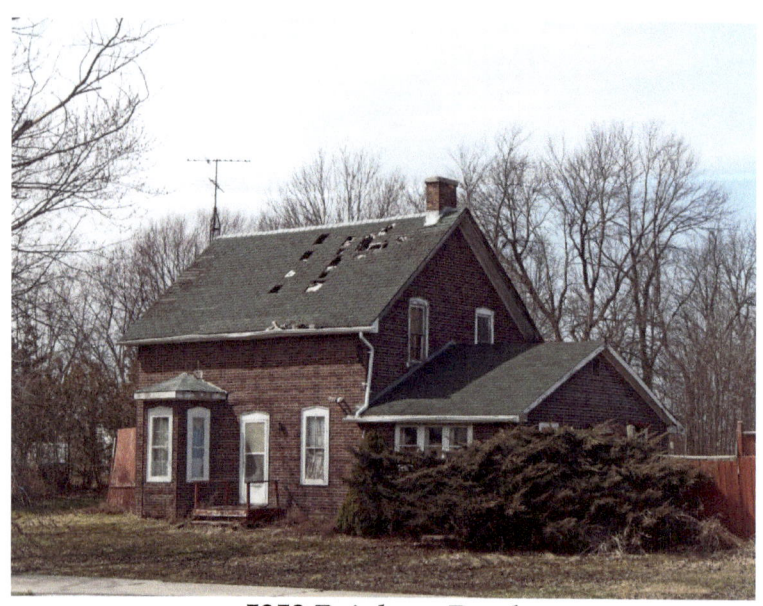

5353 Rainham Road

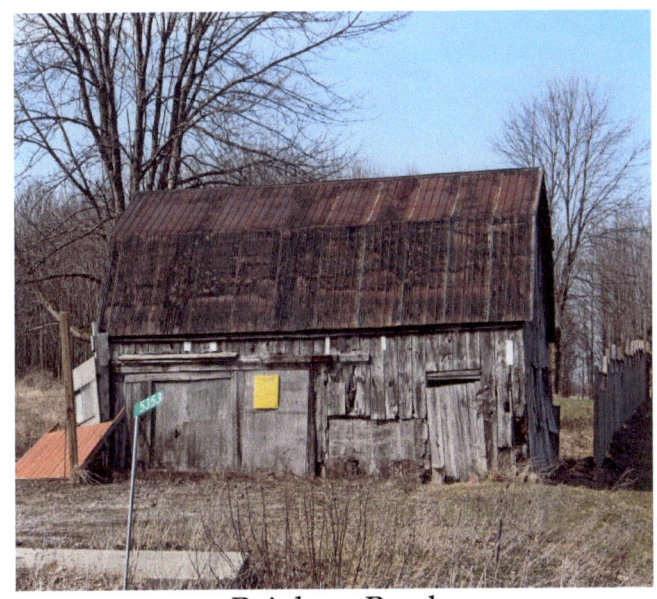

Rainham Road

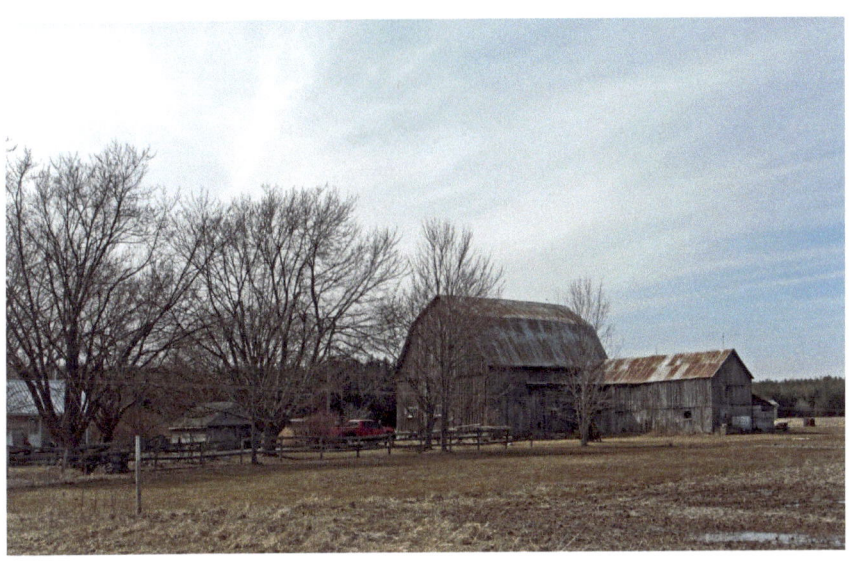

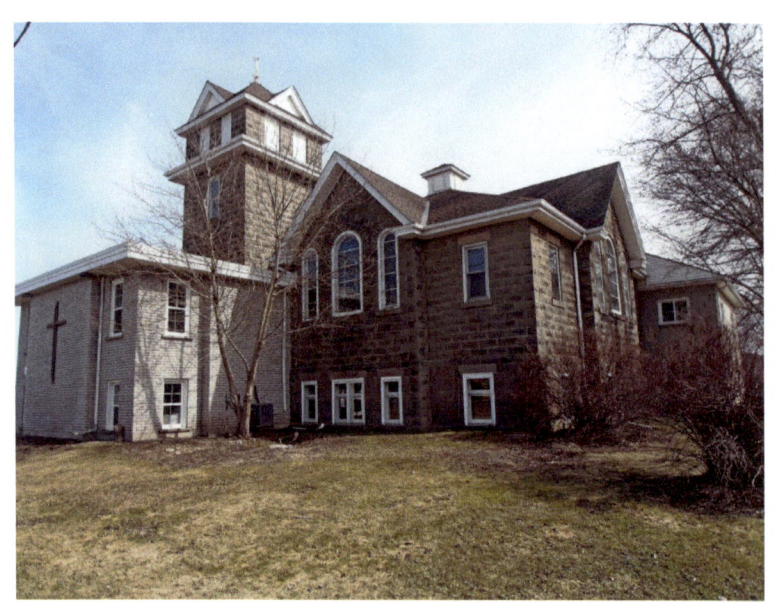

Rainham Road – Sweet's Corners Christian Church

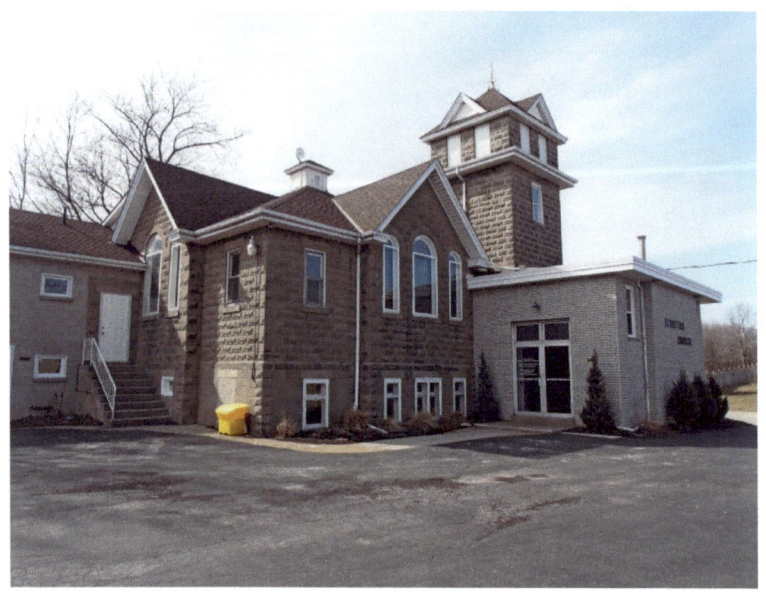

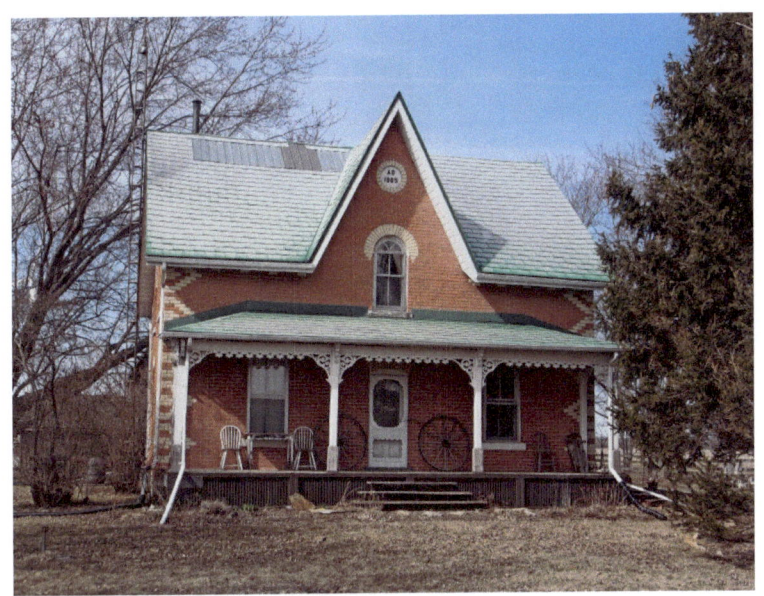

5667 Rainham Road

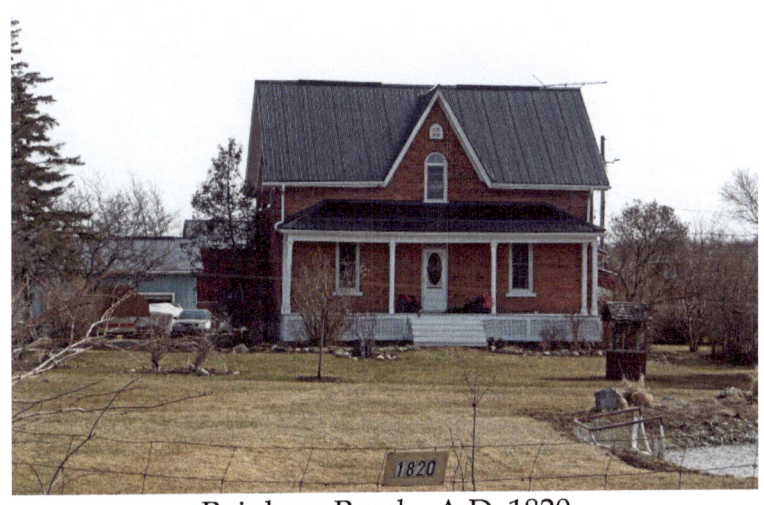

Rainham Road – A.D. 1820

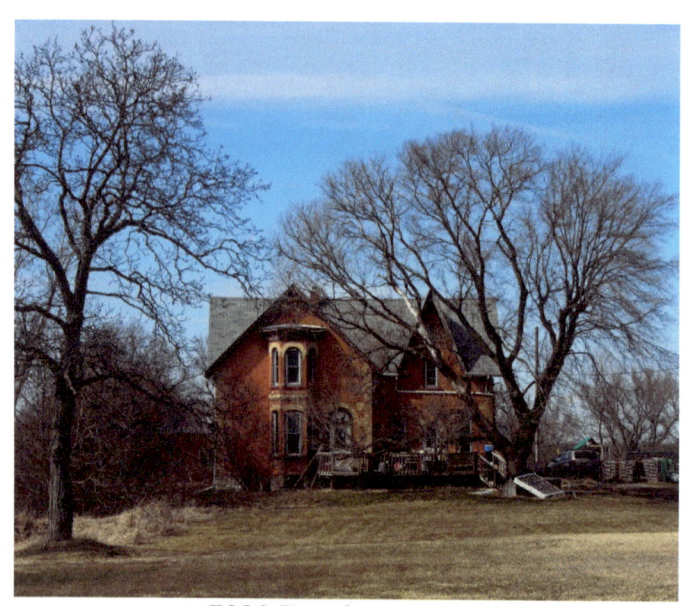

5820 Rainham Road

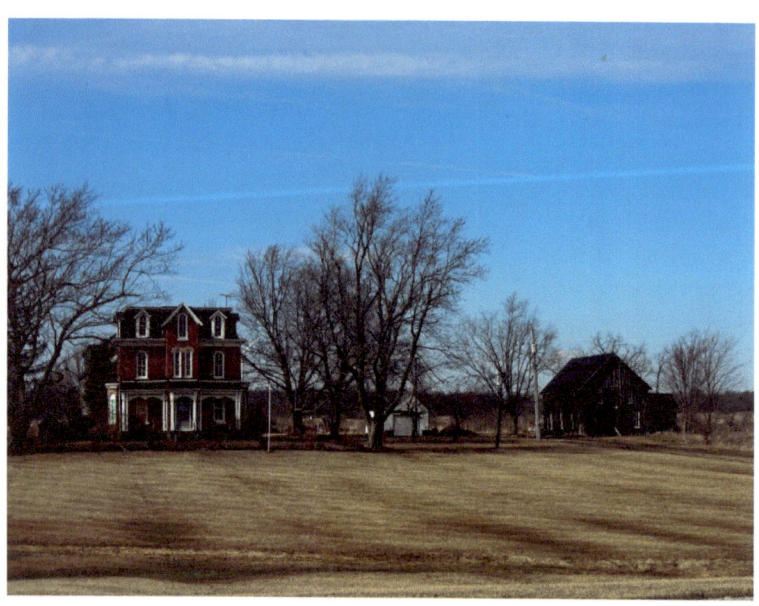

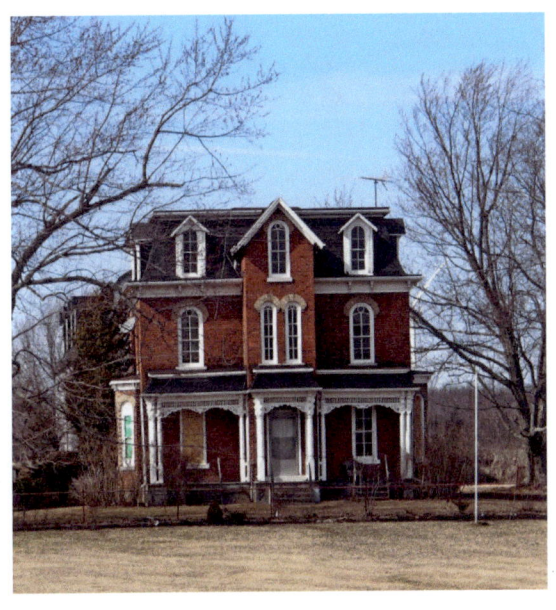

6027 Rainham Road

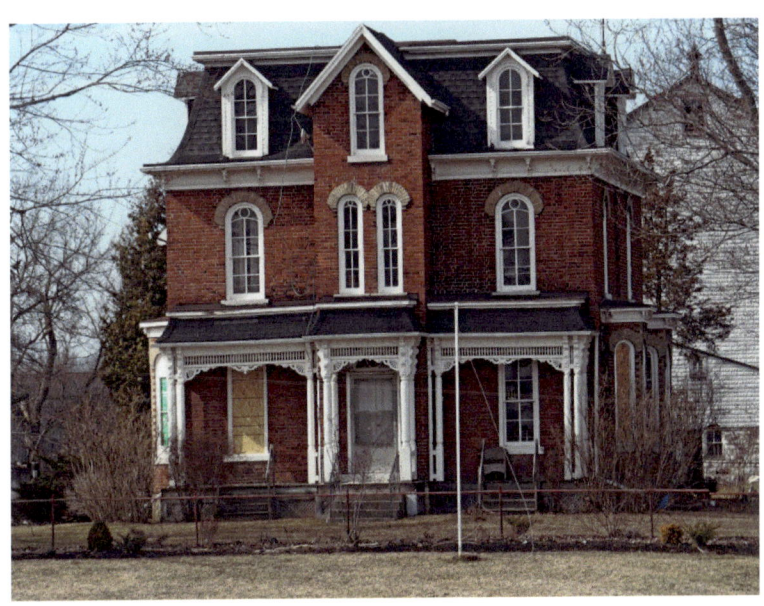

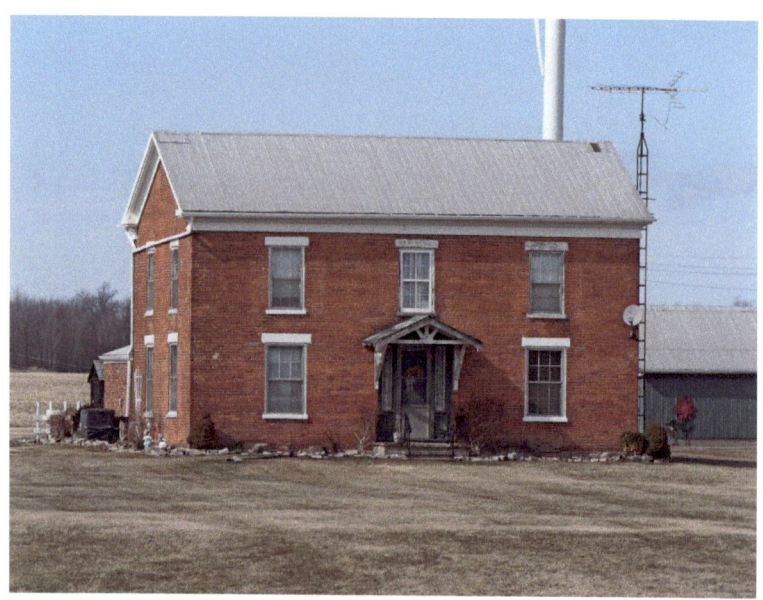

Rainham Road

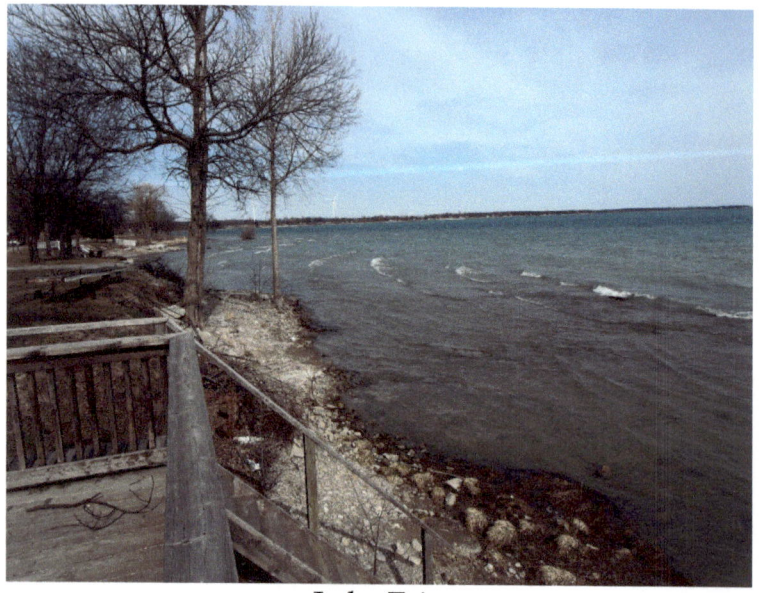

Lake Erie

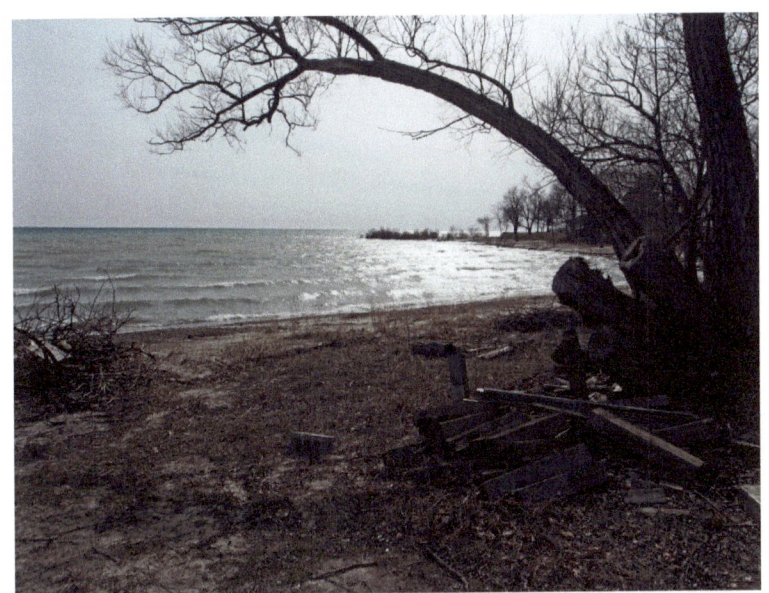
Lake Erie

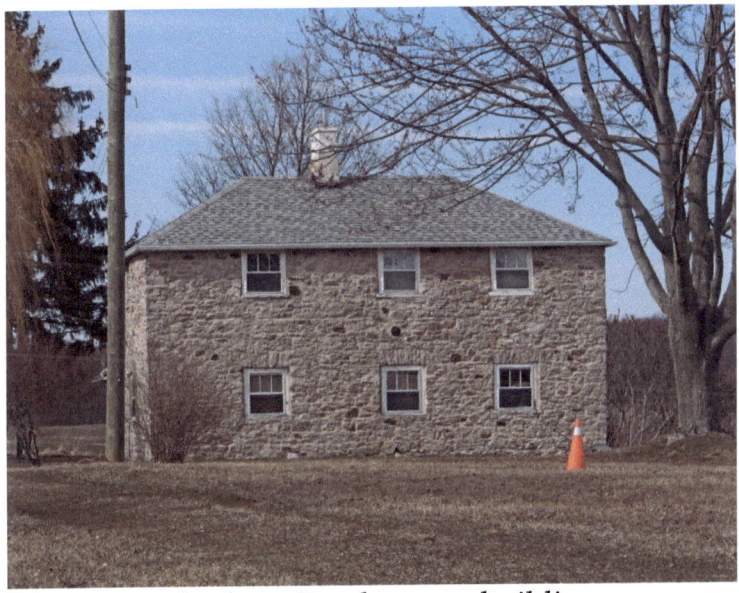
Lakeshore Road – stone building

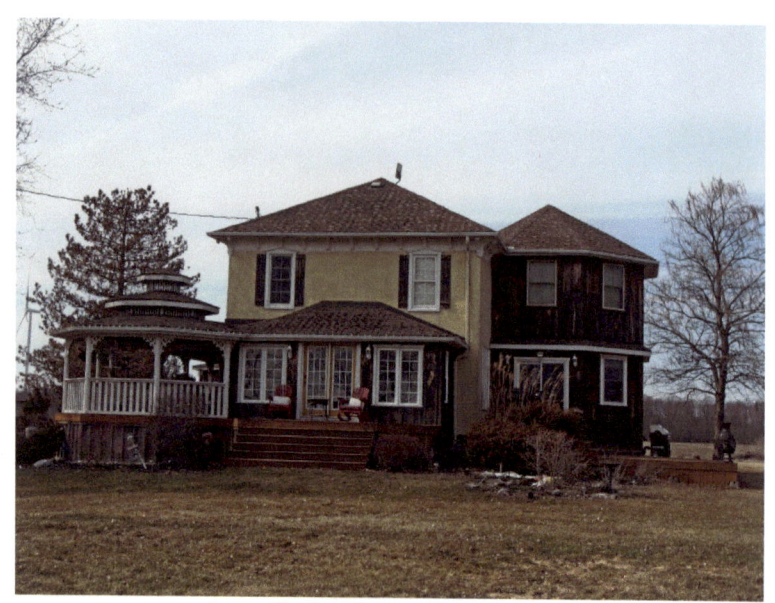

Lakeshore Road

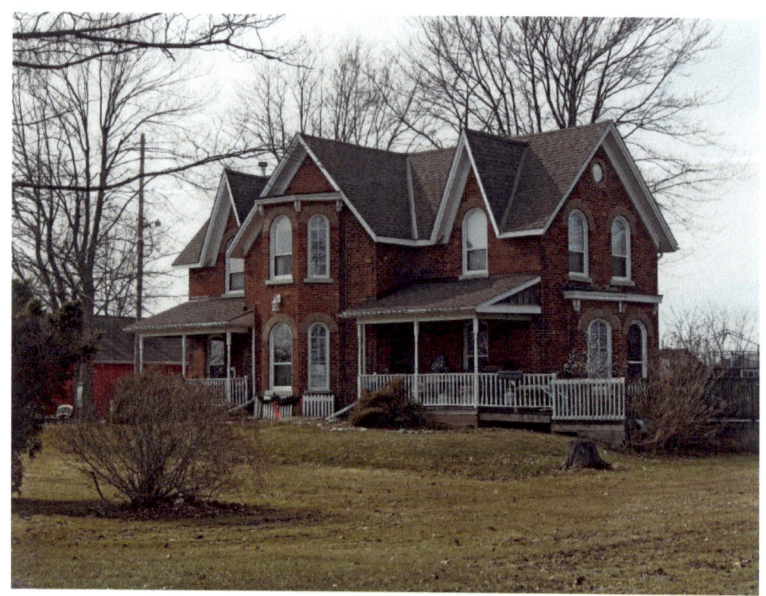

Lakeshore Road

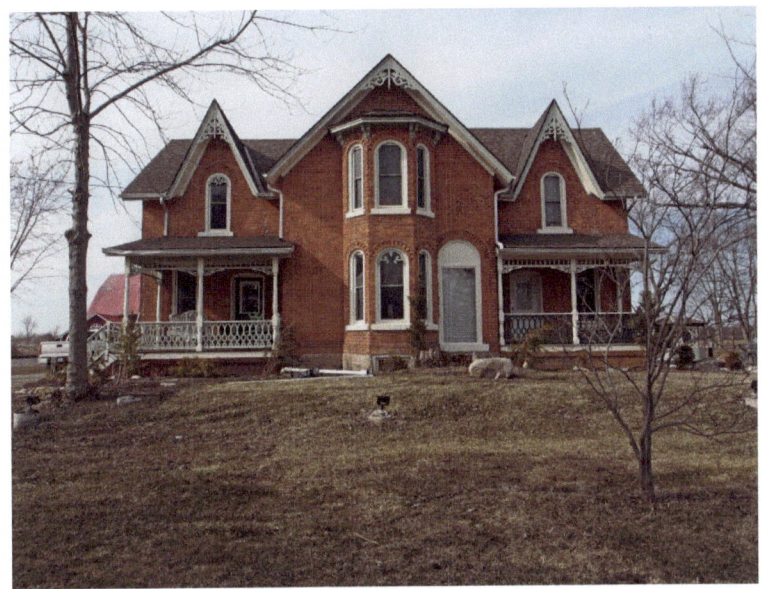

2191 Lakeshore Road

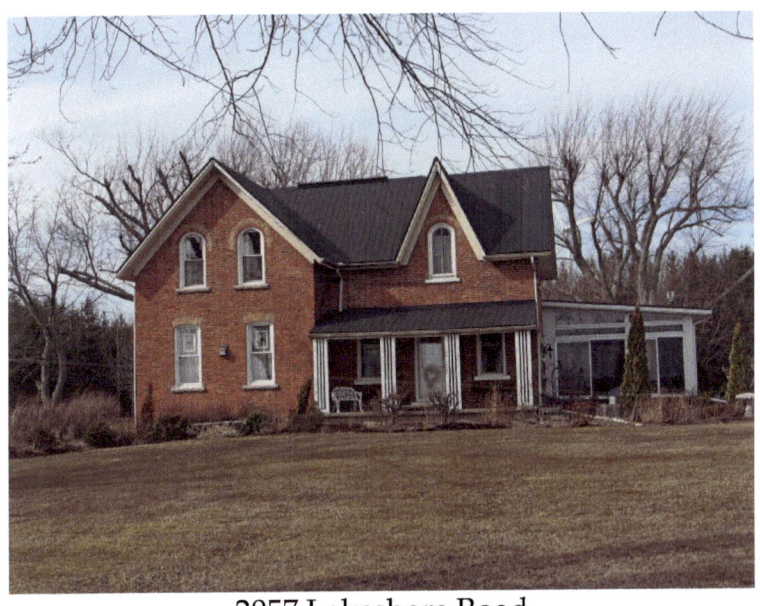

2057 Lakeshore Road

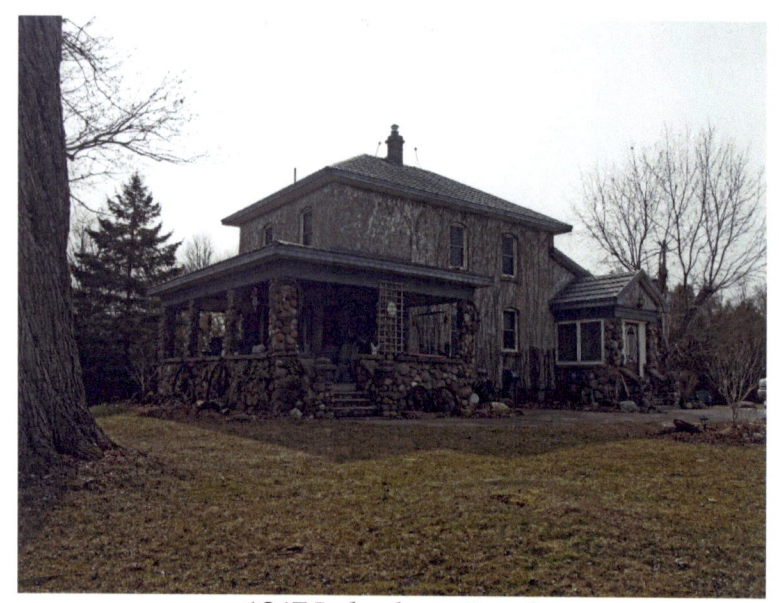

1847 Lakeshore Road

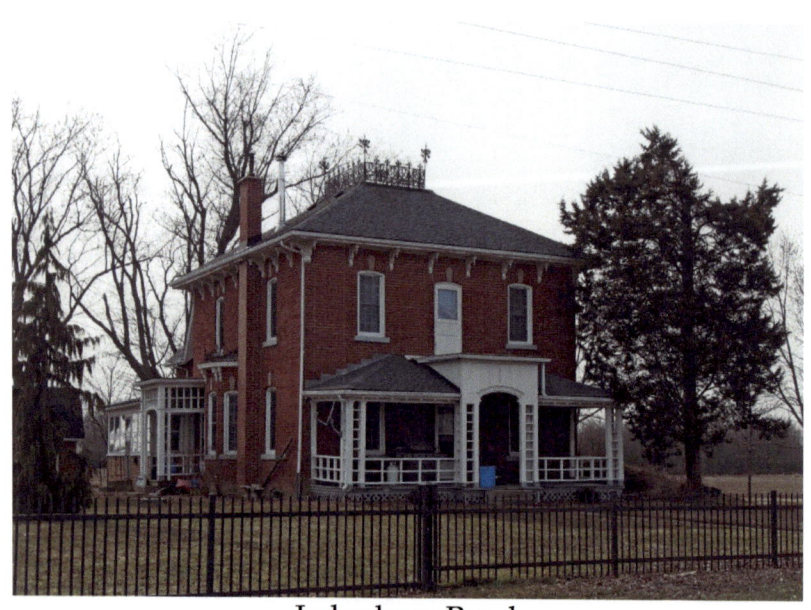

Lakeshore Road

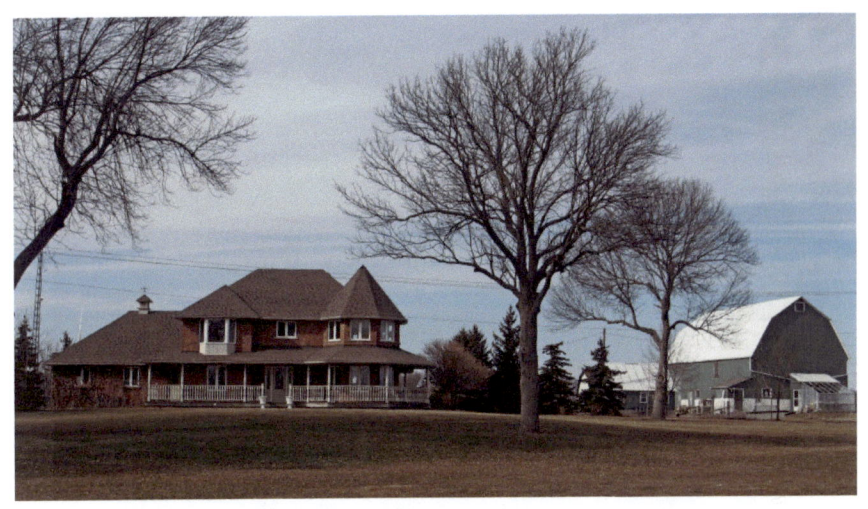

Lakeshore Road

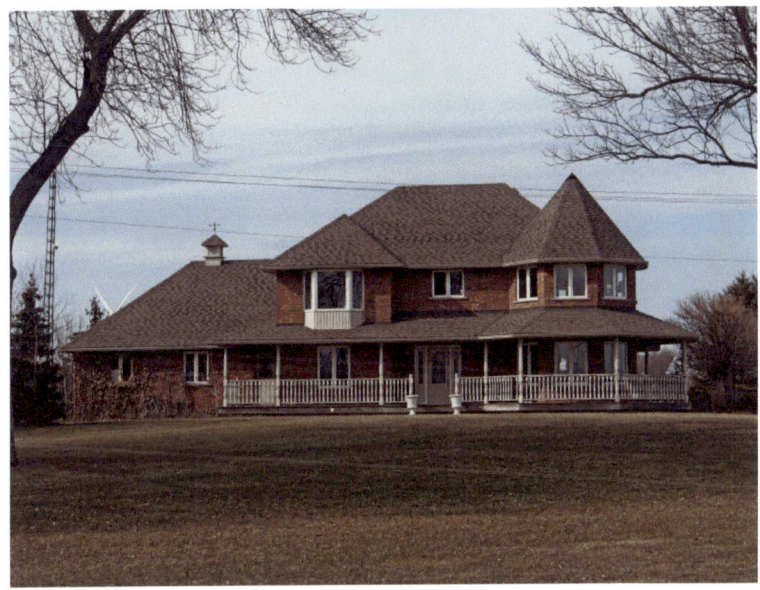

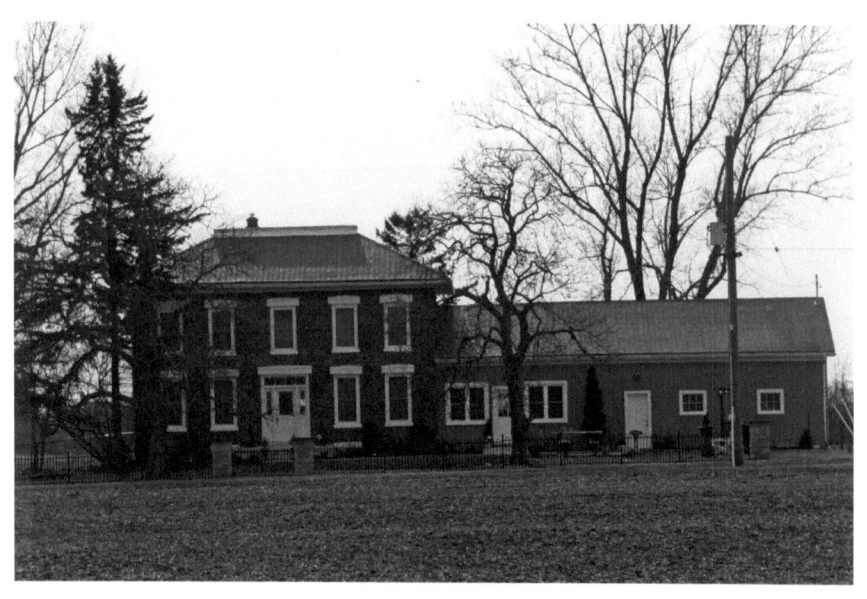

Lakeshore Road

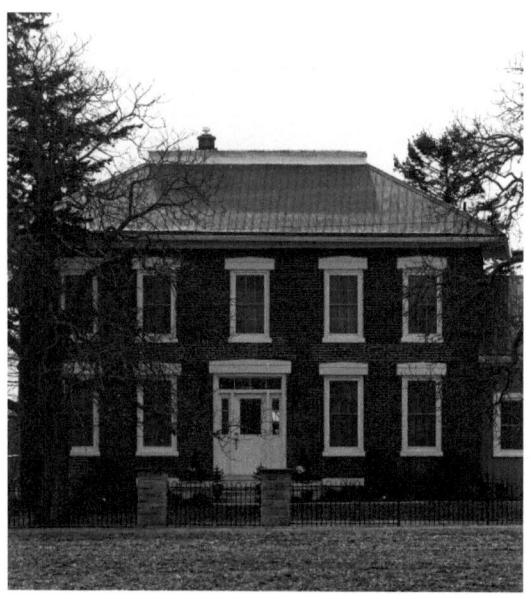

Kohler

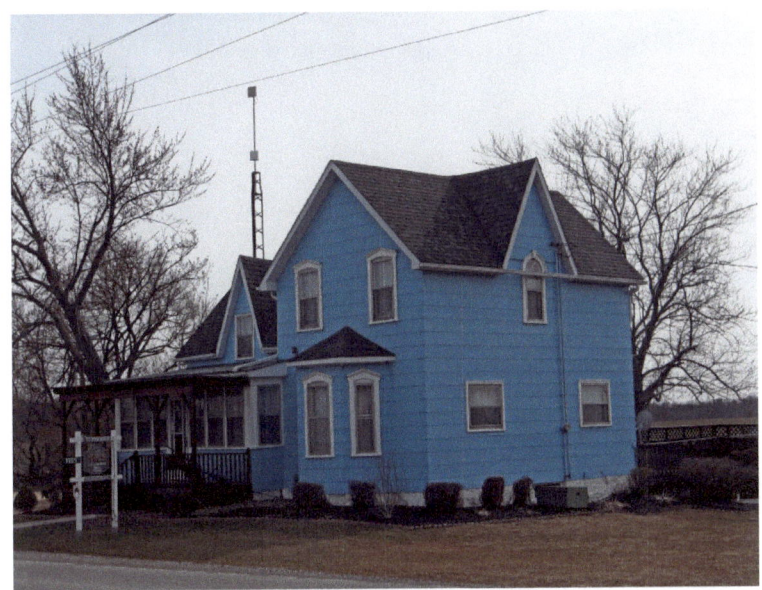

1185 Kohler Road – Gothic

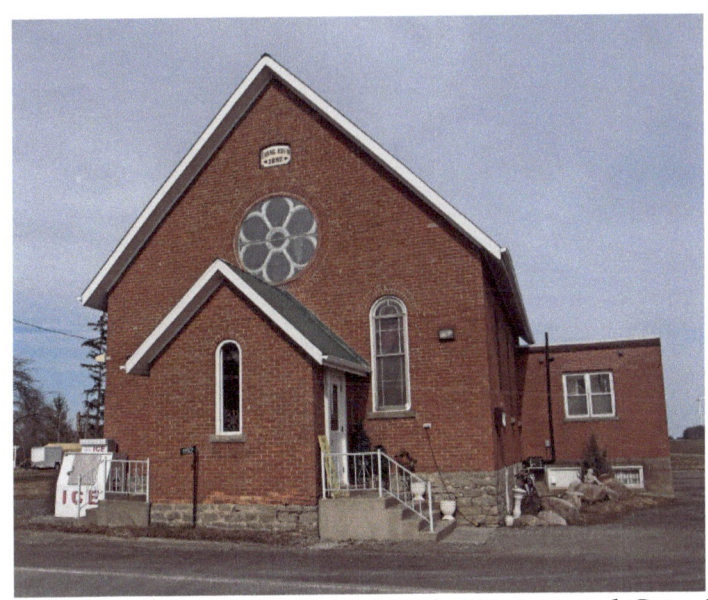

1192 Kohler Road – Shelly's Family Dining and Catering Service

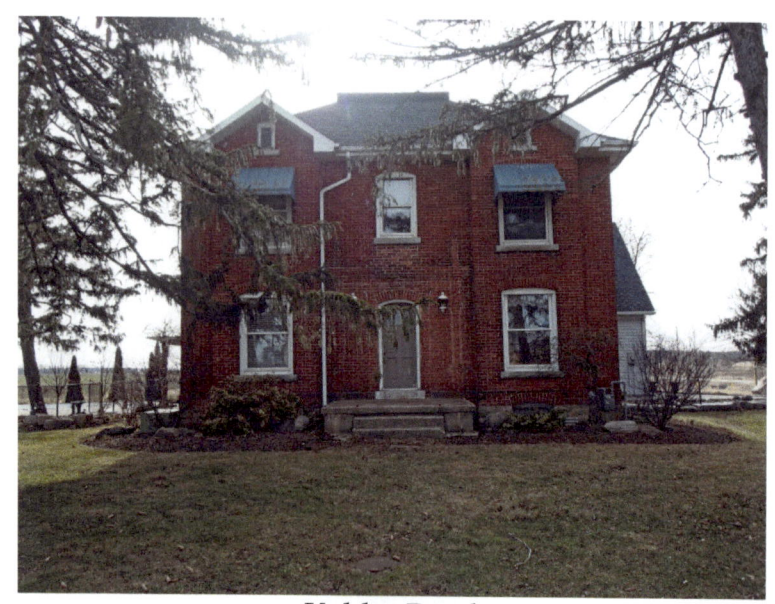

Kohler Road

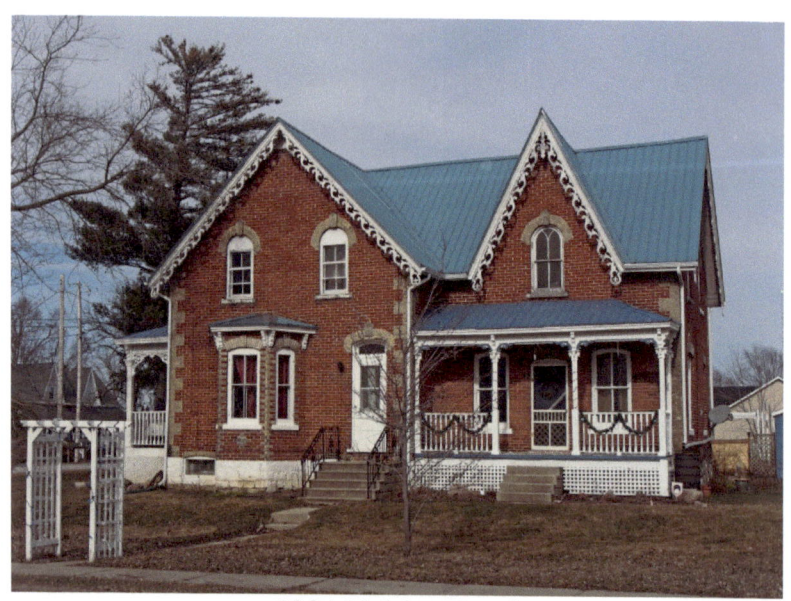

1204 Kohler Road

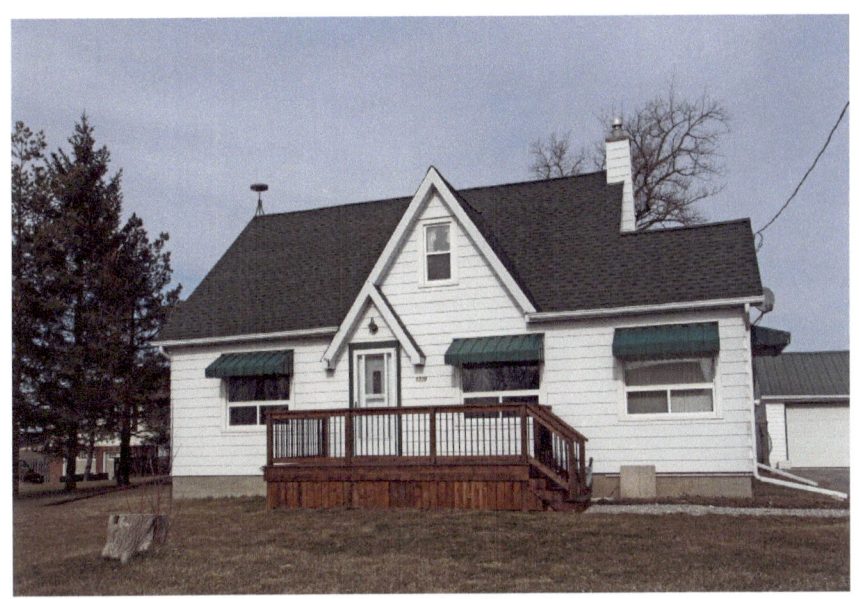

1220 Kohler Road

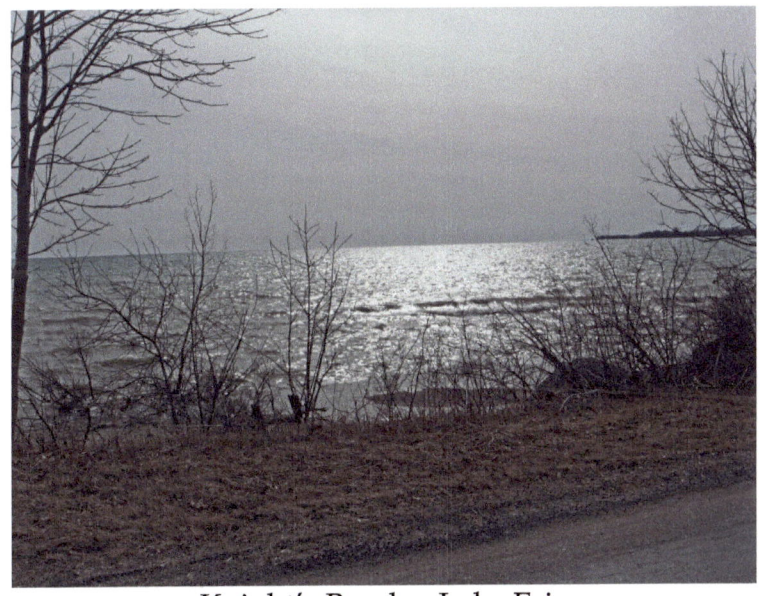

Knight's Beach – Lake Erie

Jarvis

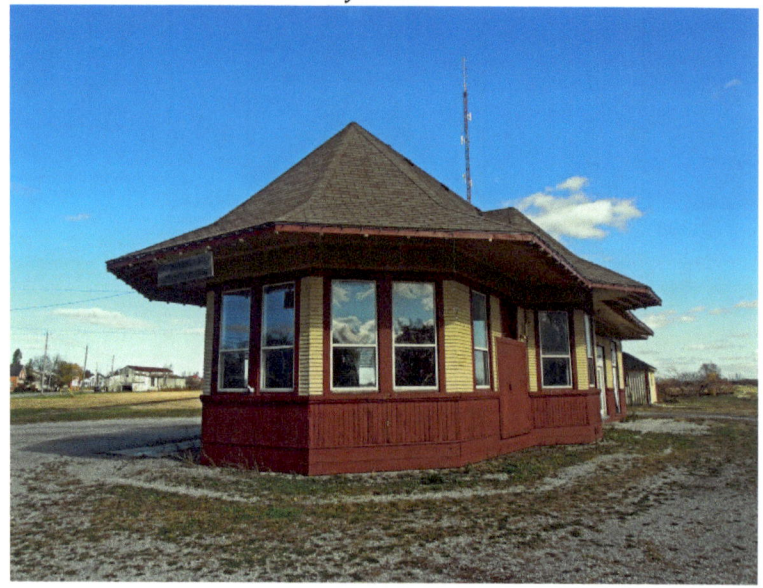

Jarvis Train Station

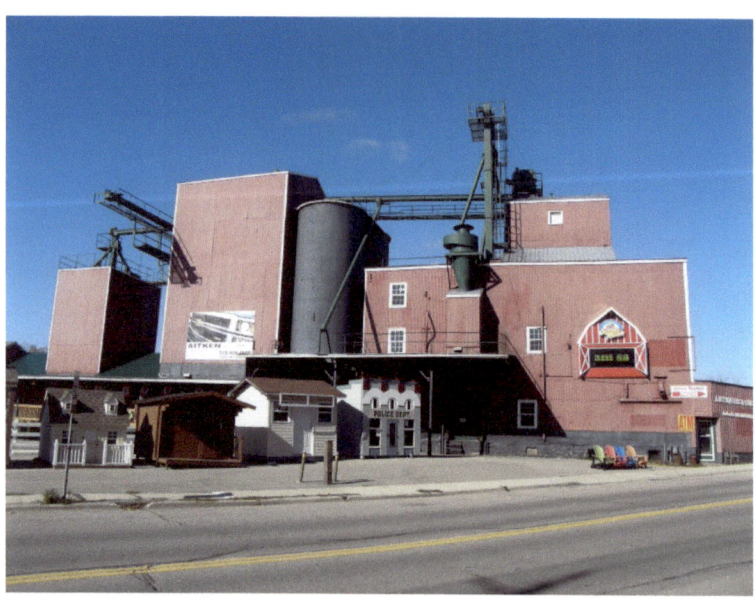

Grain elevators – now an antique market

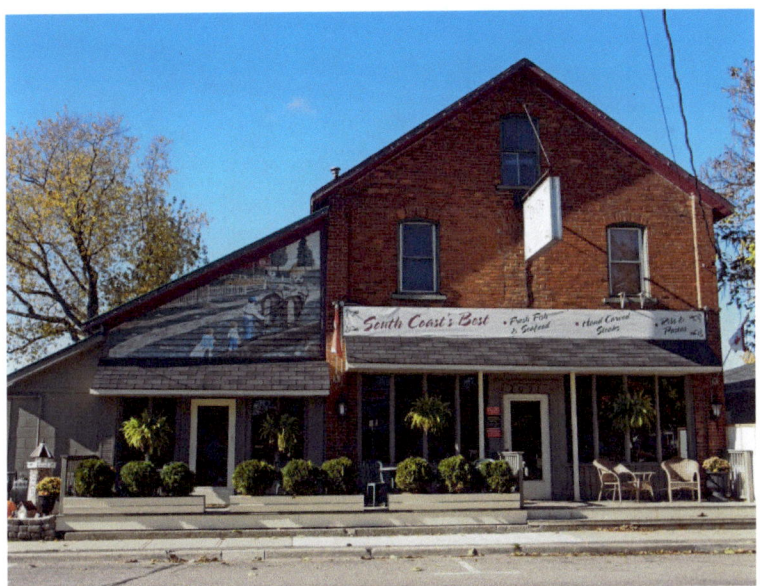

Dina D's Fine Family Dining – a great place for lunch – built in the 1880s

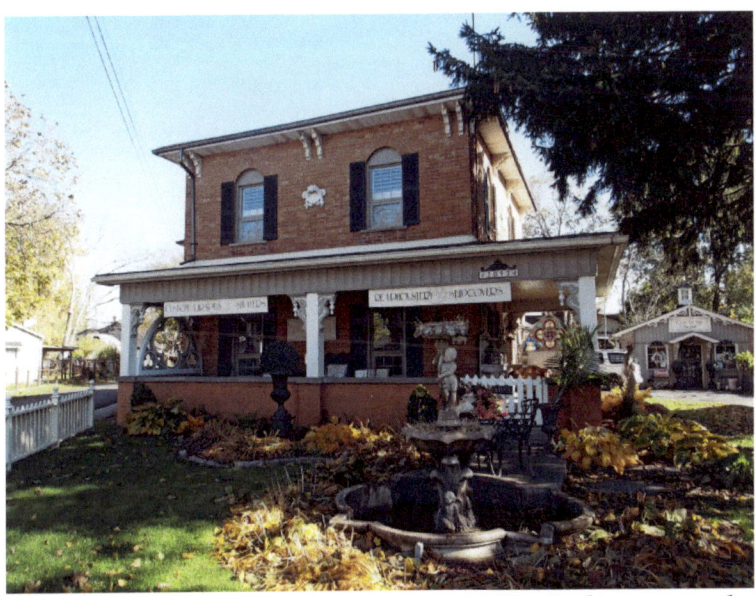

2092 Main Street – Italianate – c. 1870 - Italianate style

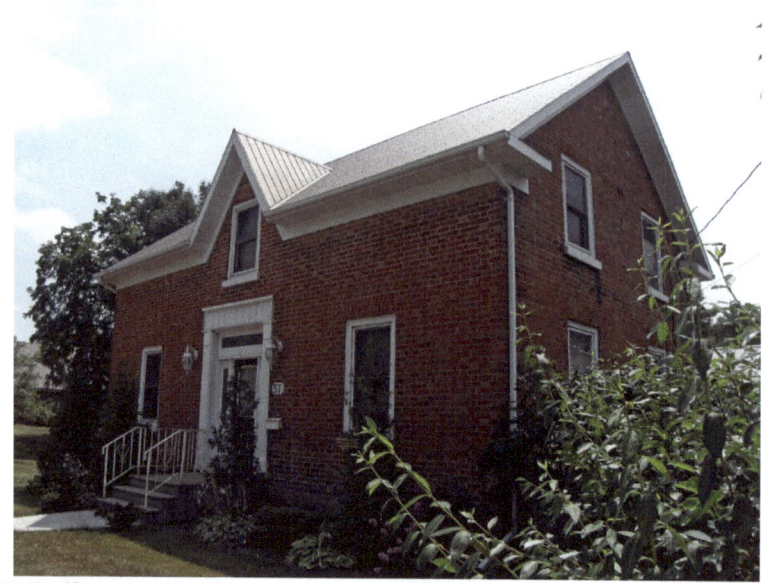

57 Talbot Street – 1½ story Gothic Revival cottage, cornice return on end gable, red brick

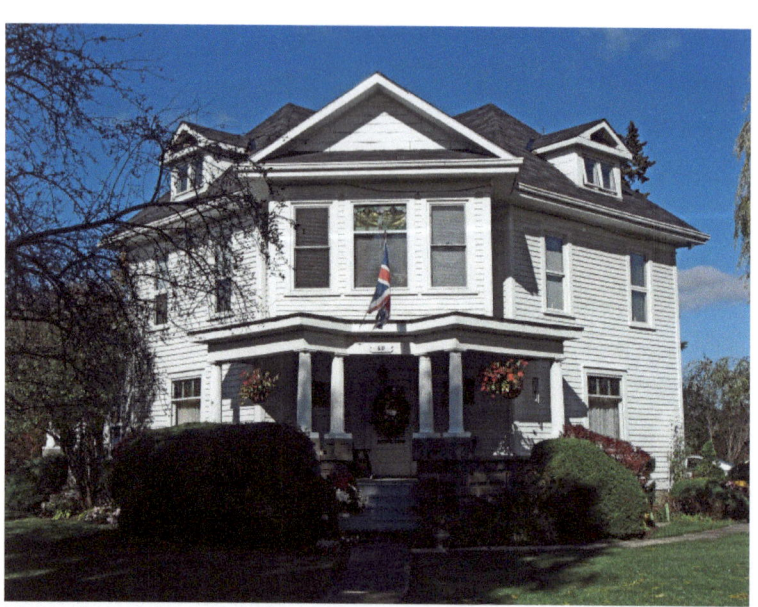

60 Talbot Street East – Italianate style with frontispiece, triangular pediment, dormers in the attic

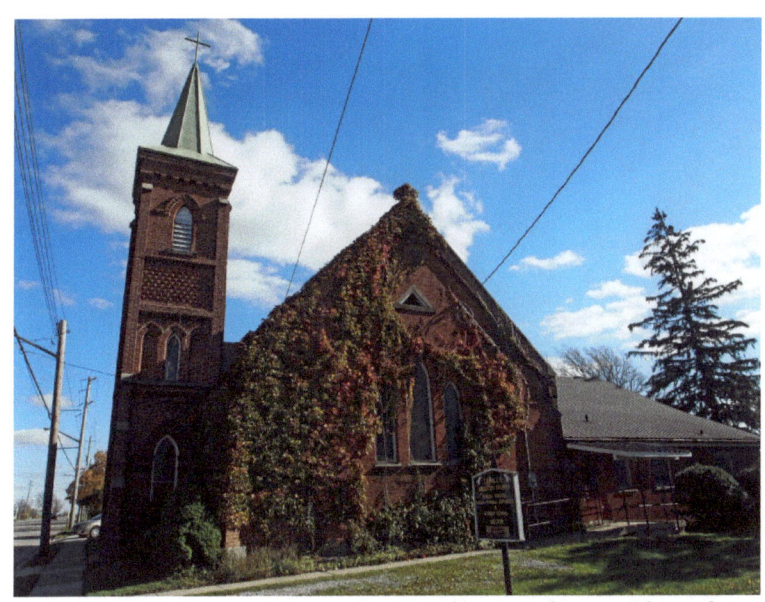

65 Talbot Street East - St. Paul's Anglican Church

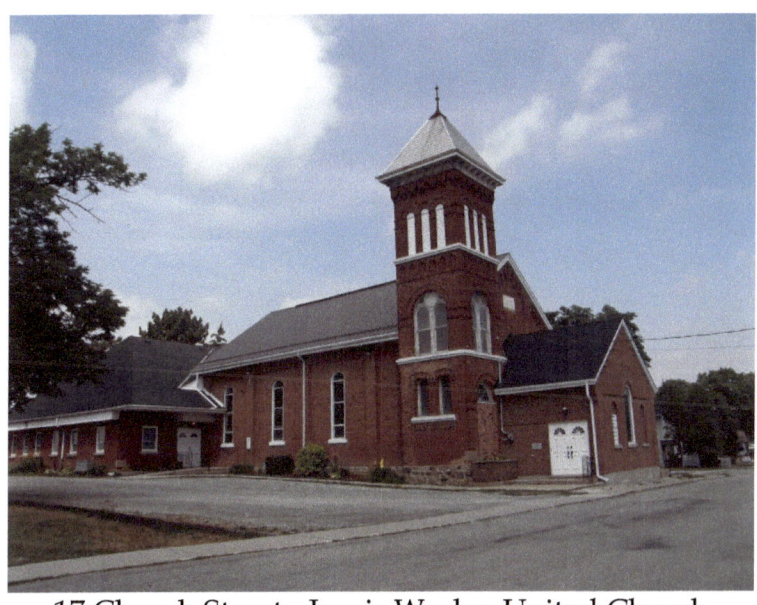

17 Church Street - Jarvis Wesley United Church

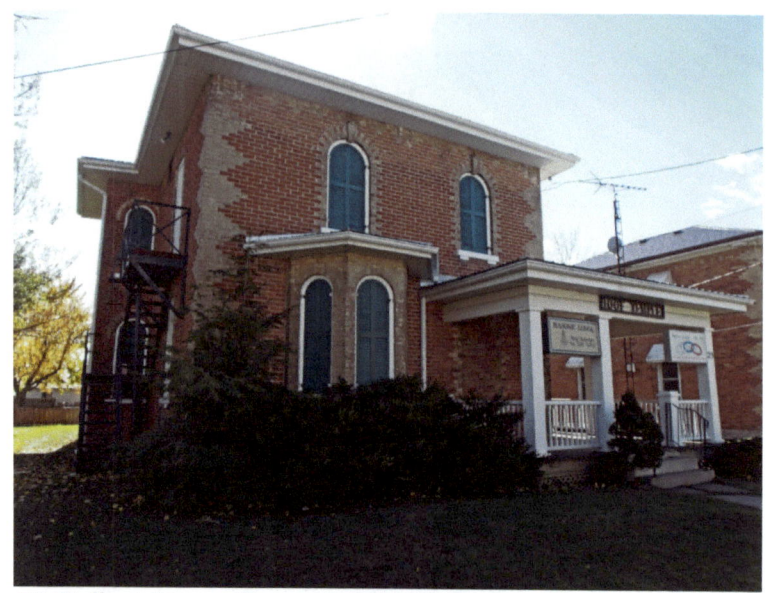

23 Talbot Street East – IOOF Temple – Masonic Lodge
Italianate style, dichromatic brickwork, bay window, keystones above windows

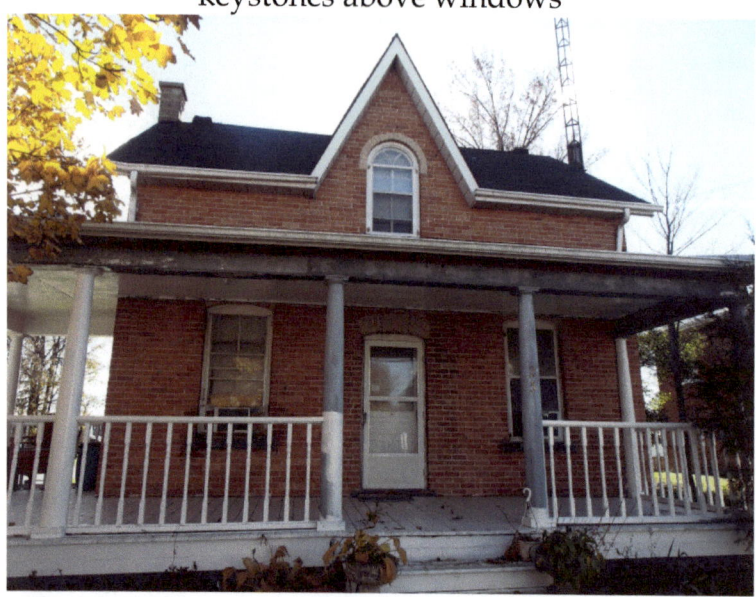

25 Talbot Street East – Gothic cottage, dichromatic brickwork, buff-coloured window hoods

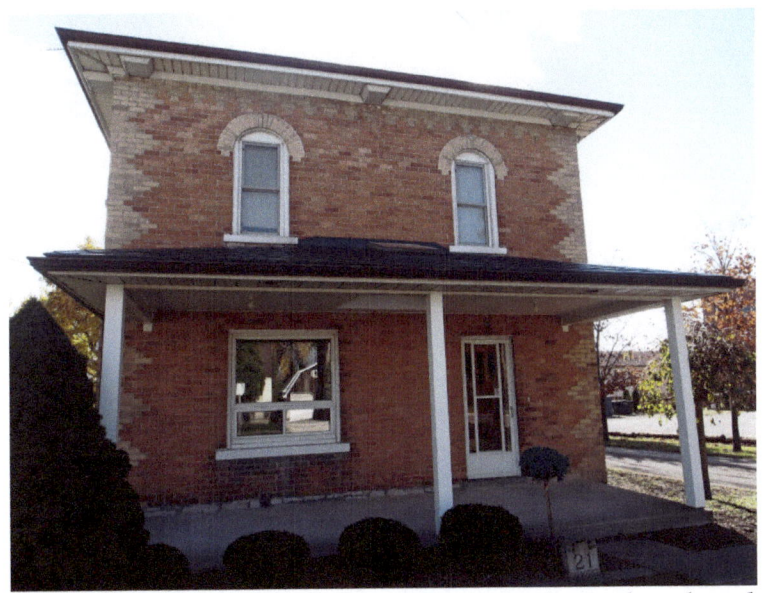

21 Talbot Street – Italianate style, arched window hoods

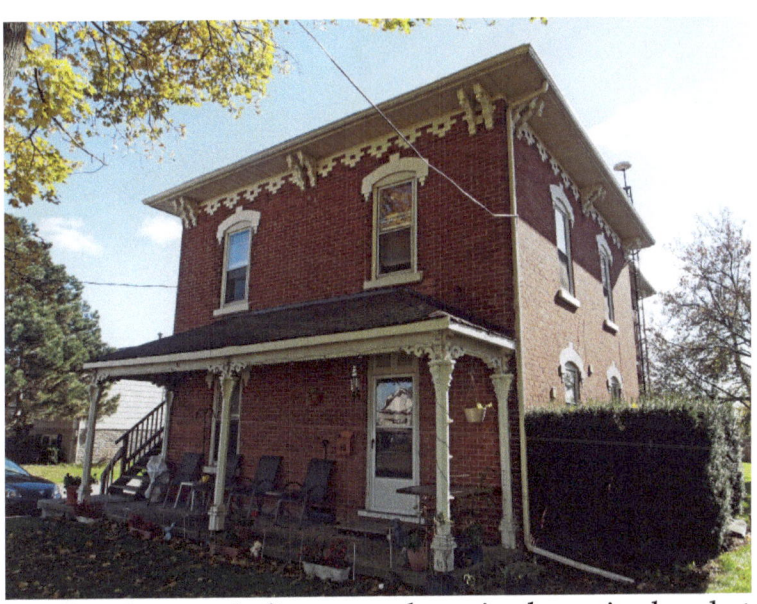

53 Talbot Street – Italianate style, paired cornice brackets, dichromatic patterning below cornice, arched window hoods

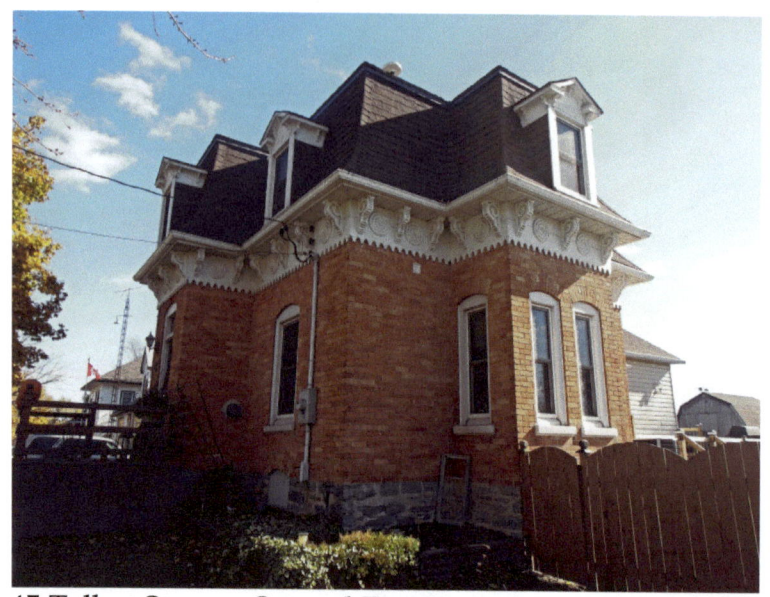

45 Talbot Street – Second Empire style – mansard roof, dormers in roof, single cornice brackets, cornice return on small gables on window dormers

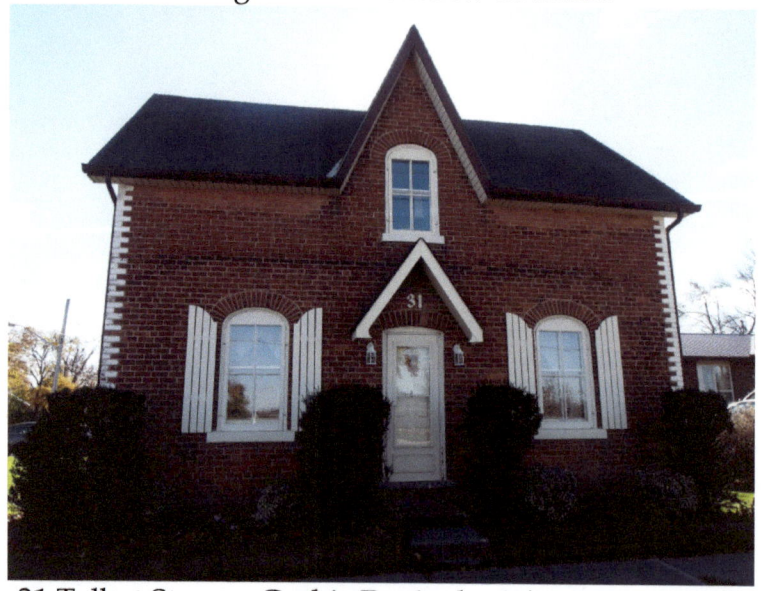

31 Talbot Street – Gothic Revival – 1½ stories, arched voussoirs

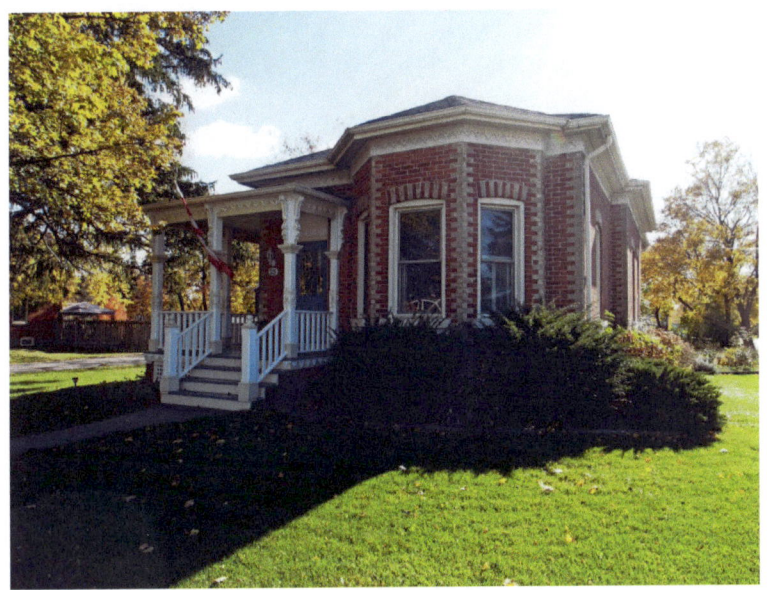

25 Talbot Street – dichromatic brickwork, corner quoins – Italianate style – unusual one floor only

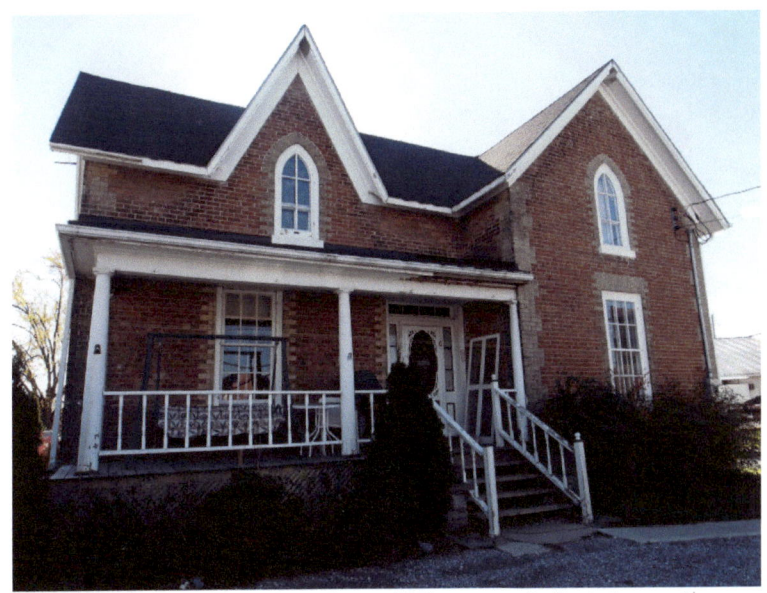

Gothic Revival style – dichromatic brickwork

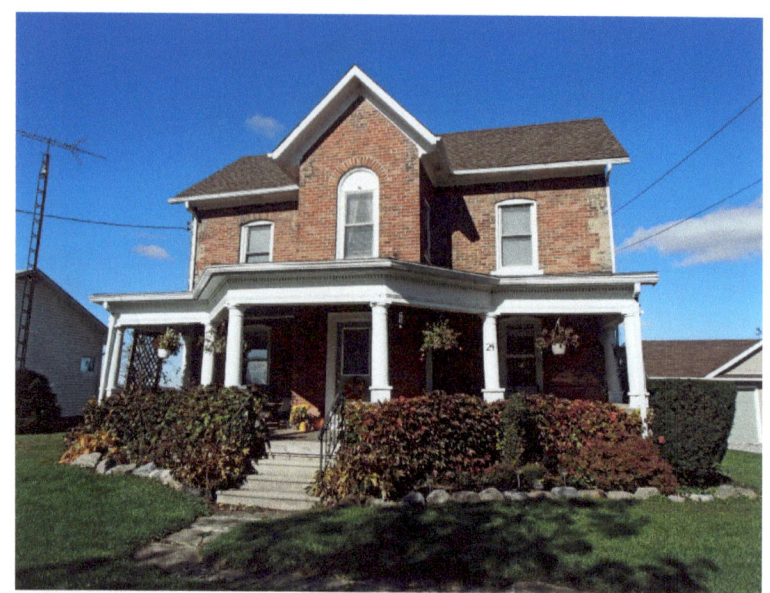

24 Talbot Street – Gothic Revival style – red brick, corner quoins

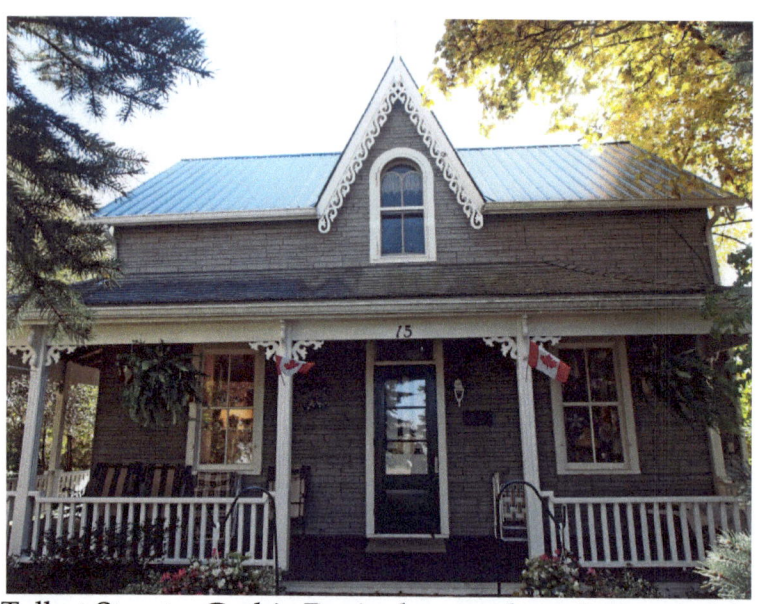

15 Talbot Street – Gothic Revival, verge board trim and finial on gable

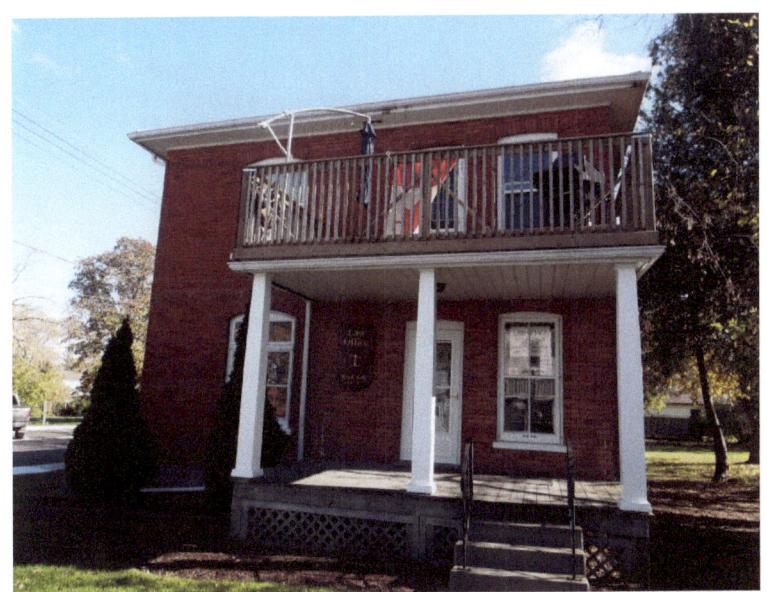

Italianate style

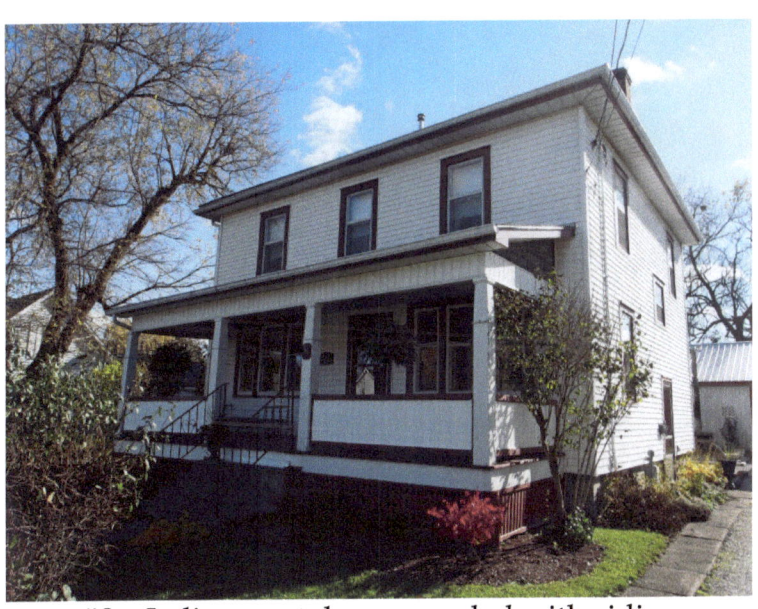

#8 – Italianate style – upgraded with siding

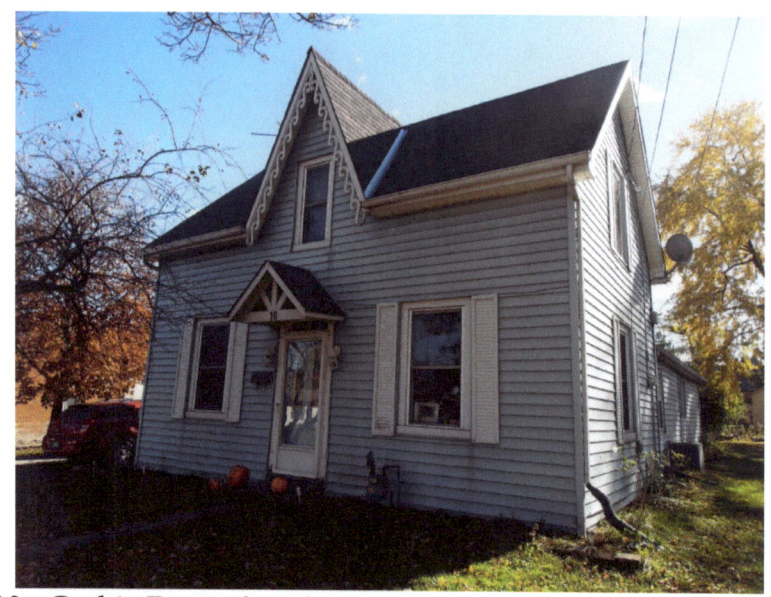

#10 - Gothic Revival with verge board trim on the attic gable

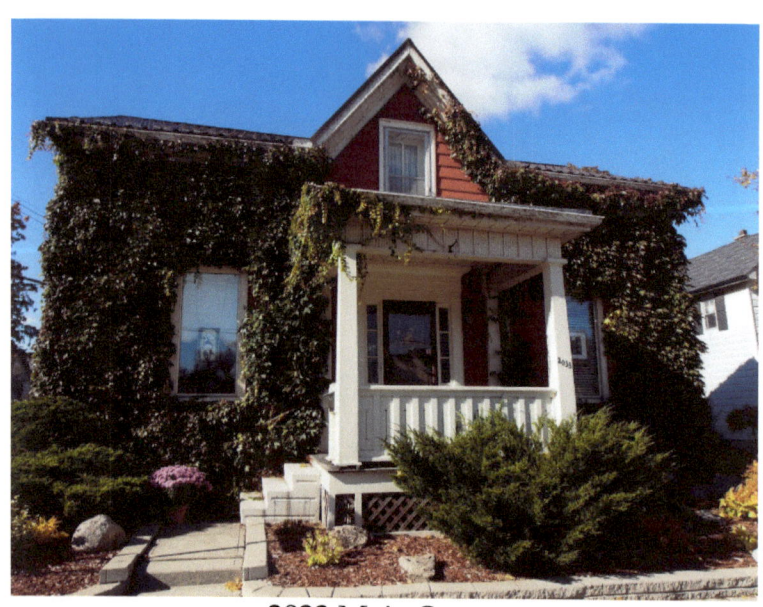

2033 Main Street

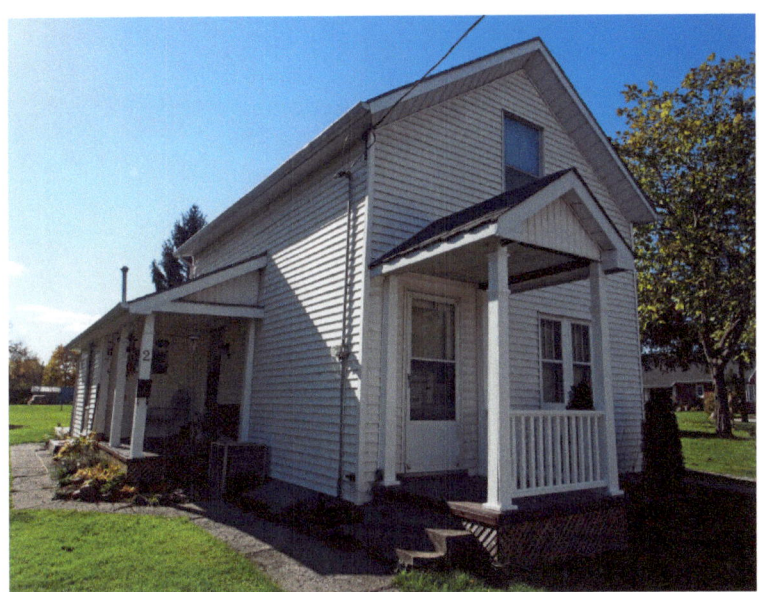

2 Peel Street

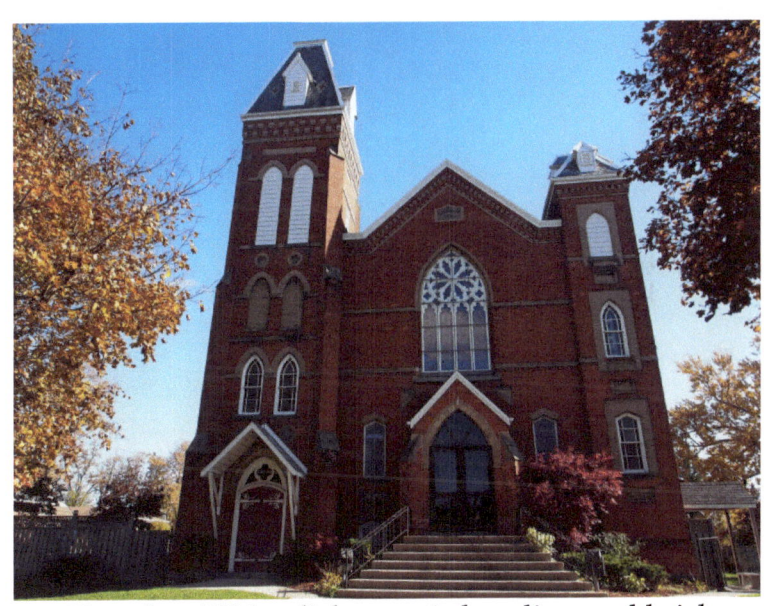

Knox Church – 1896 – dichromatic banding and brickwork, dichromatic tile work in tower

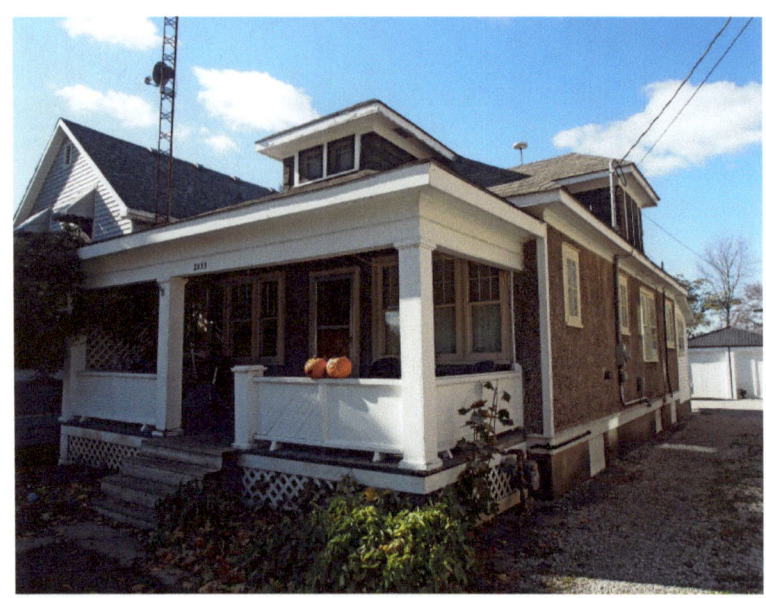

2055 Main Street – Italianate – dormer in roof – stucco exterior

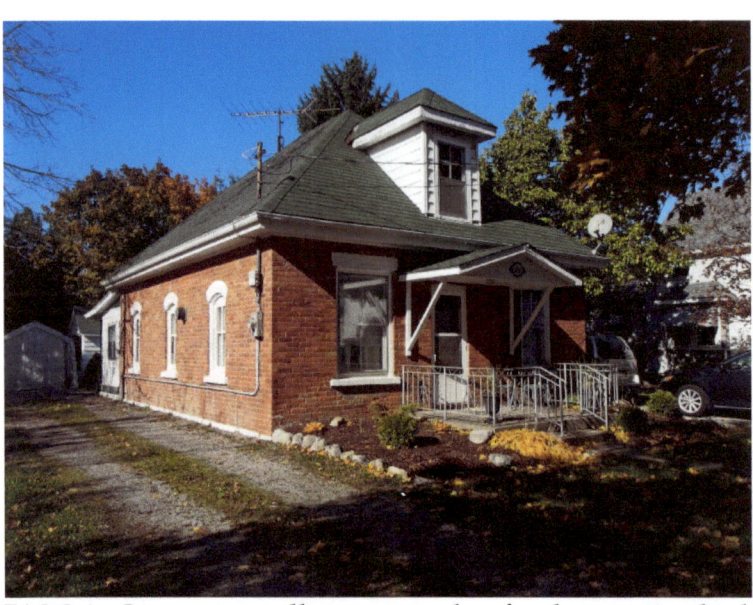

2051 Main Street – excellent example of a dormer in the hip roof – Italianate style

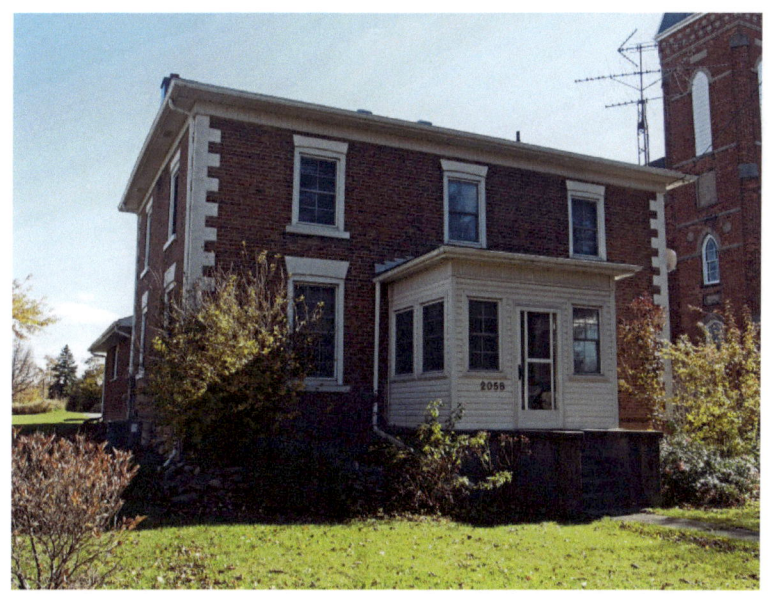

2058 Main Street – Italianate style, dichromatic brickwork

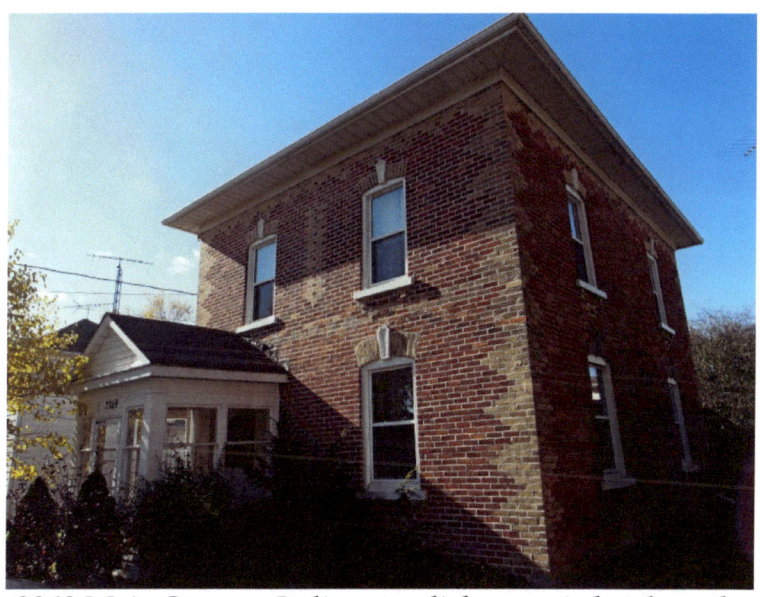

2069 Main Street – Italianate, dichromatic brickwork, voussoirs with keystones

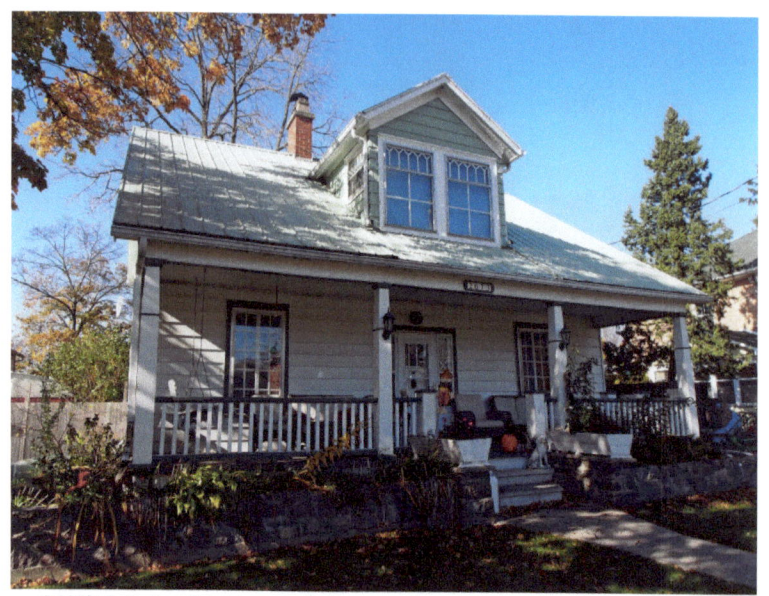

2073 Main Street – dormer in attic – Gothic cottage

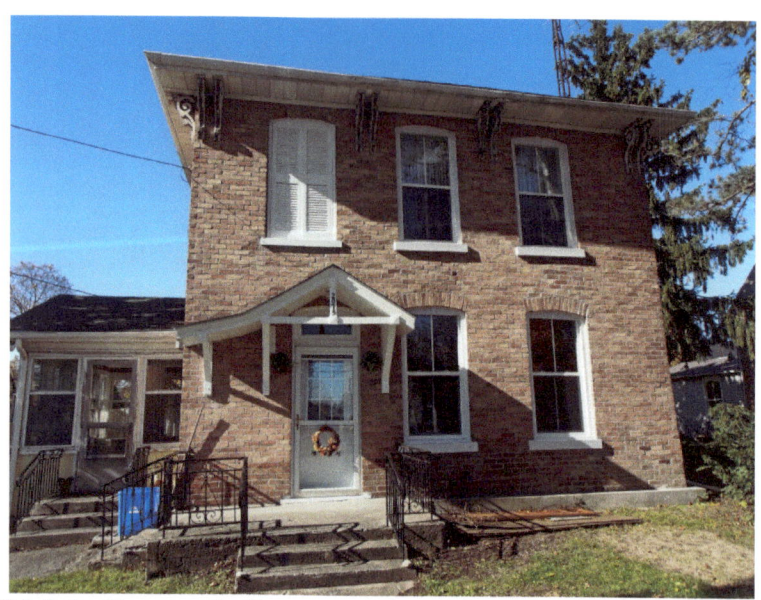

2075 Main Street – Italianate style with paired cornice brackets

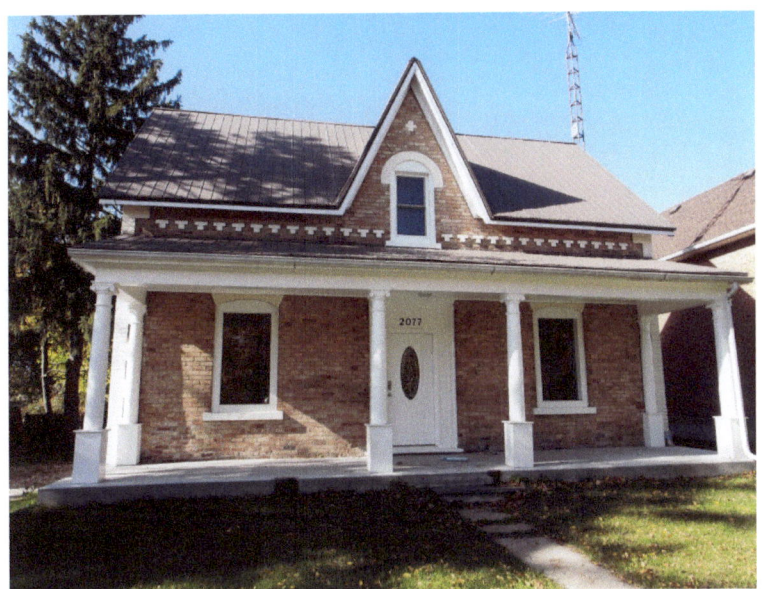

2077 Main Street – arched window hood in attic gable – Gothic cottage, light red brick, decorative brickwork below cornice

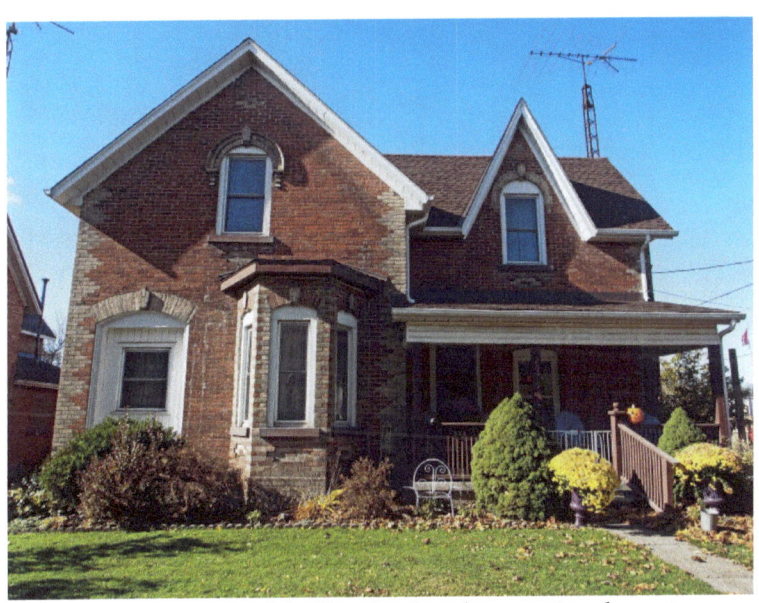

2079 Main Street - Gothic Revival – decorative keystones and voussoirs, bay window, dichromatic brickwork

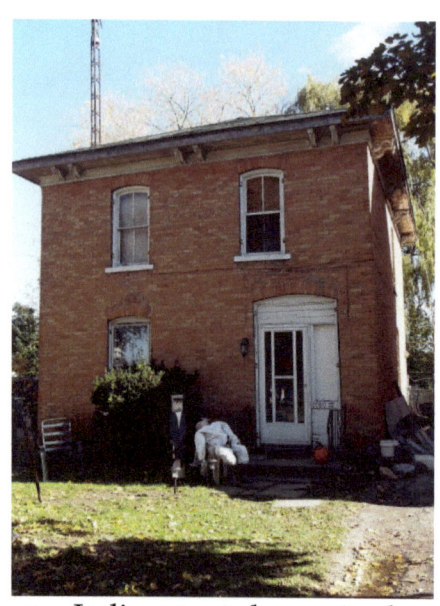

2080 Main Street – Italianate style – paired cornice brackets, orange/red brick

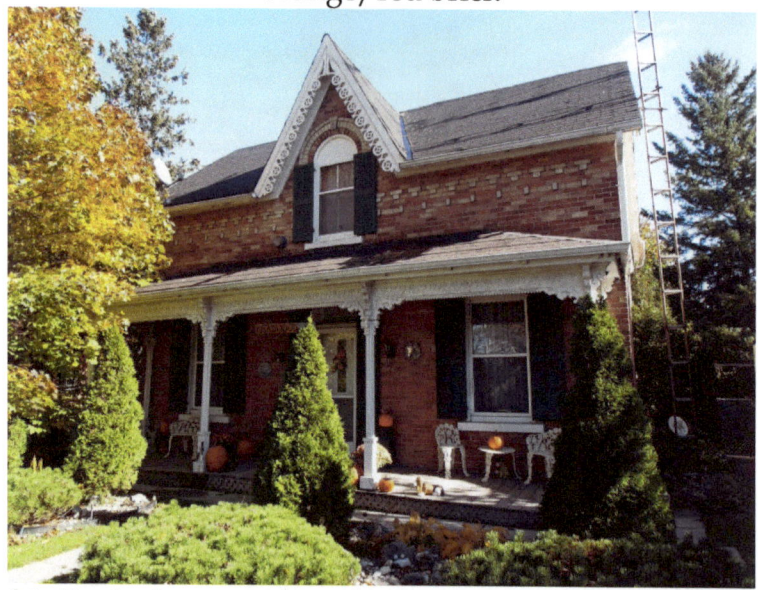

Gothic Revival – verge board trim on gable, arched voussoirs and keystones, orange/red brick, decorative brickwork below cornice – "Meadwood"

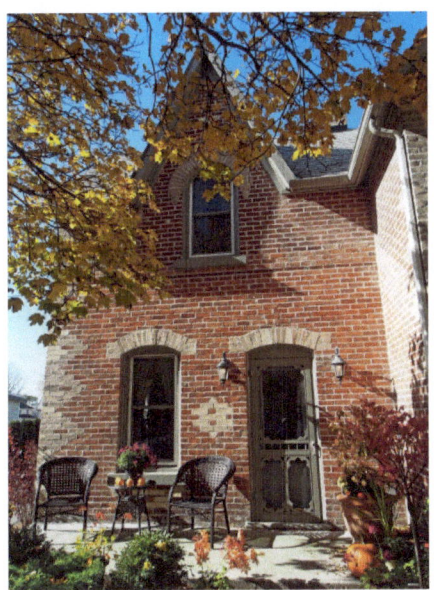

Gothic Revival – dichromatic brickwork

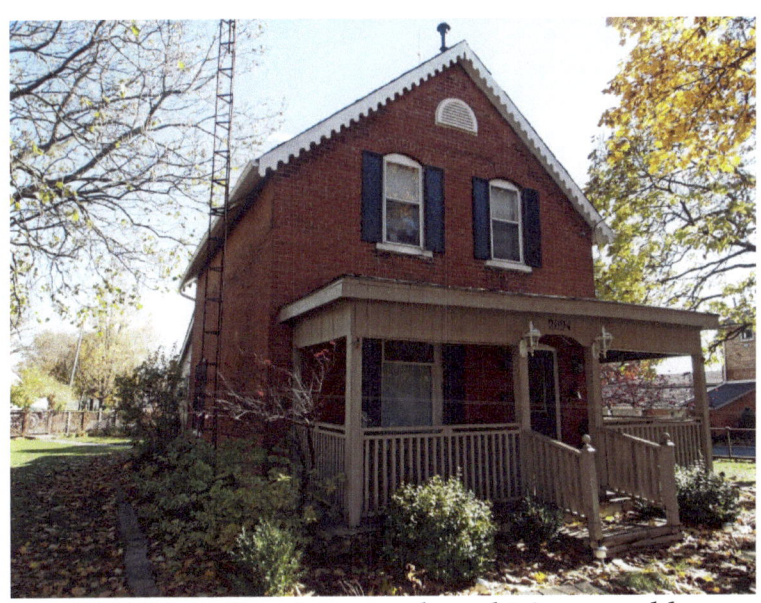

2094 Main Street – verge board trim on gable

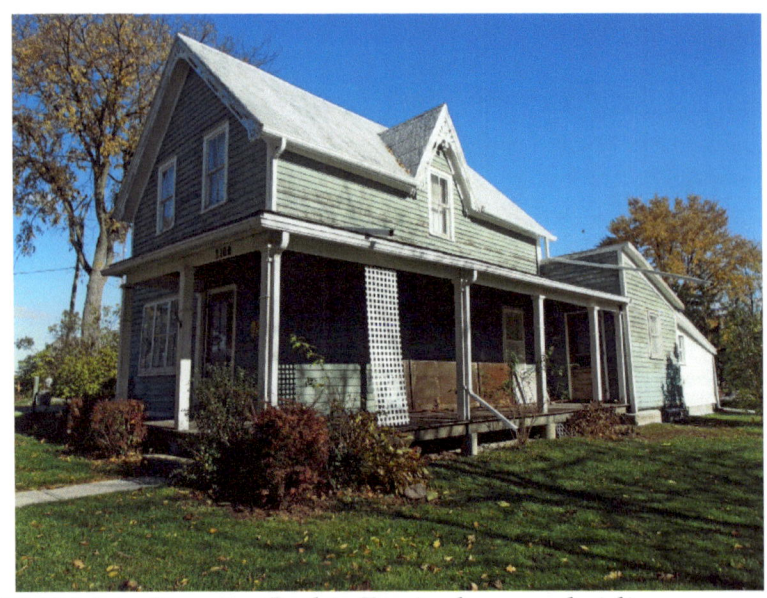

2100 Main Street – Gothic Revival – wood siding – verge board trim on gables

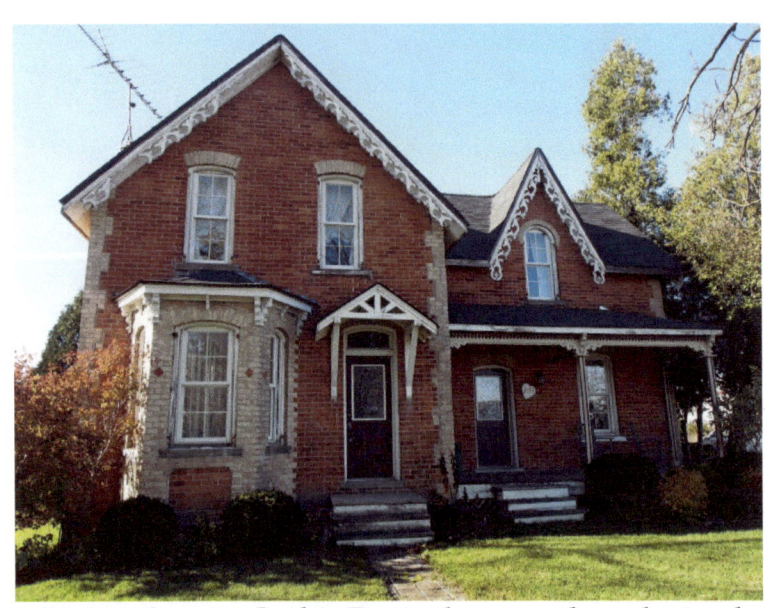

2145 Main Street - Gothic Revival – verge board trim, bay window with cornice brackets

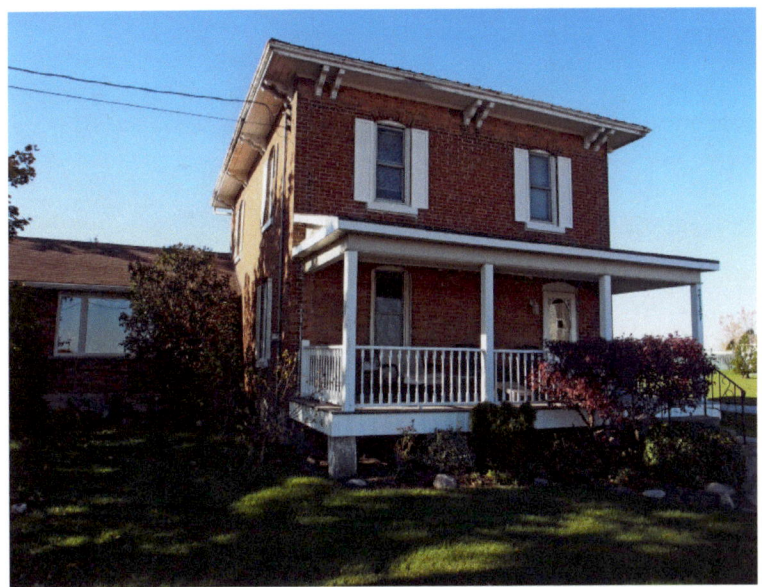

2137 Main Street – Italianate

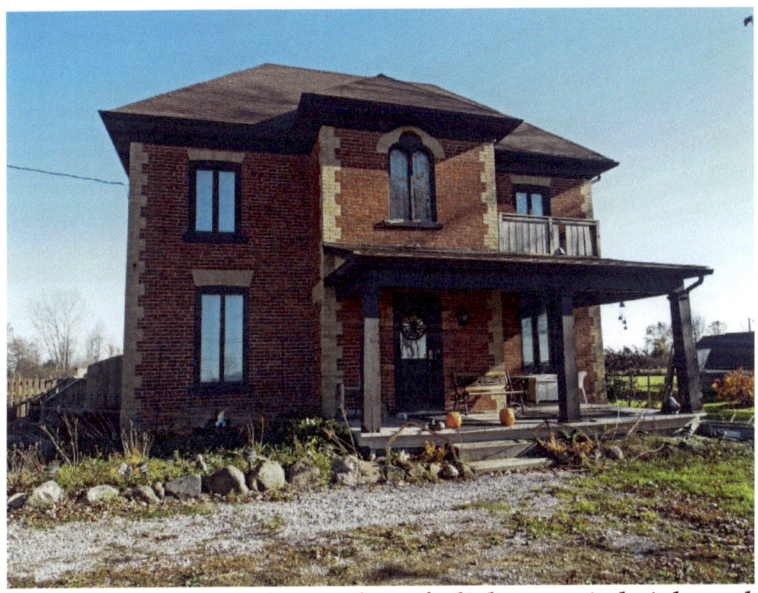

c. 1847 – Italianate, hipped roof, dichromatic brickwork

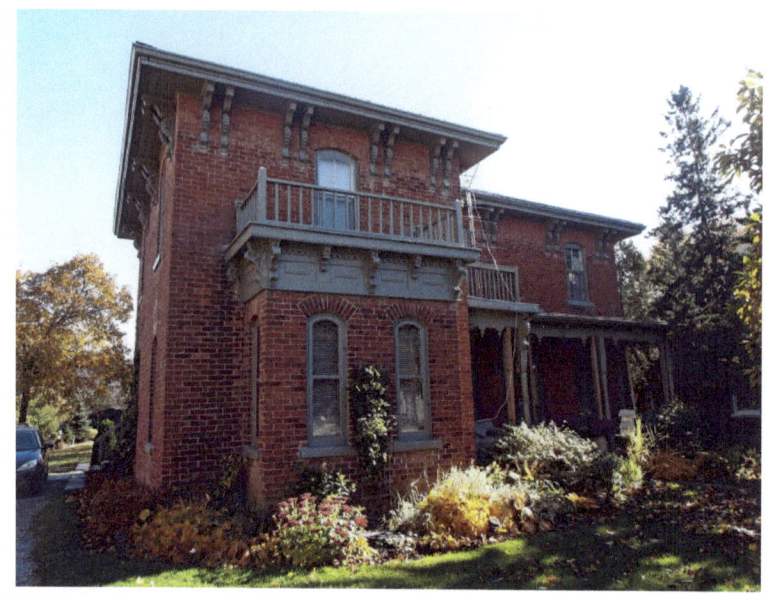

2086 Main Street – Italianate – paired cornice brackets, arched voussoirs, red brick

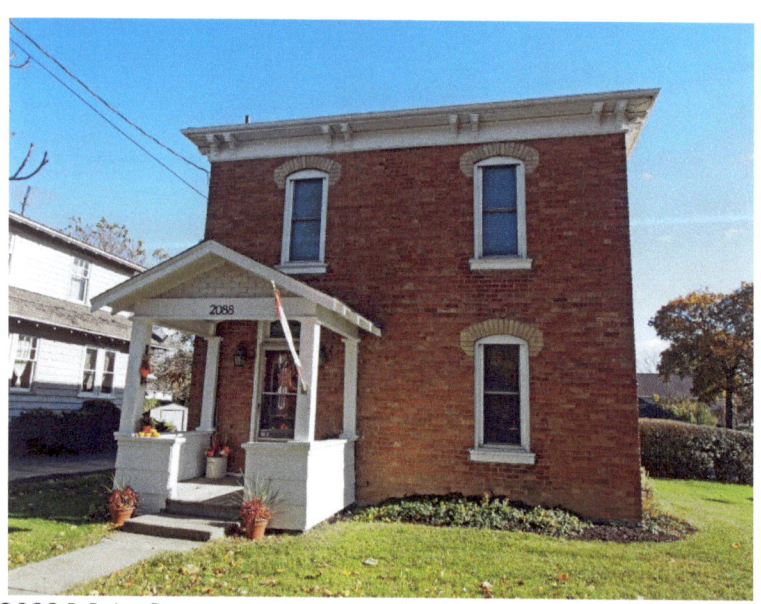

2088 Main Street – two story, Italianate, arched window hoods, paired cornice brackets

Building Styles

Georgian, before 1860 – This style began with the British King Georges in the 18th century. These buildings have balanced facades around a central door, medium-pitched gable roofs, and small paned windows.

Gothic Revival, 1830-1890 – These decorative buildings have sharply-pitched gables with highly detailed verge boards, pointed-arch window openings, and dichromatic brickwork. It is a common style in Ontario.

Italianate, 1850-1900 – A two story rectangular building with a mild hip roof, a projecting frontispiece, and generous eaves with ornate cornice brackets was the basis of the style; often there are large sash windows, quoins, ornate detailing on the windows, belvederes and wraparound verandahs. Italianate commercial buildings often have cast iron cresting and elegant window surrounds.

Romanesque Revival, 1880-1910 – This style hearkens back to medieval architecture of the 11th and 12th centuries with a heavy appearance, blocky towers and rounded arches.

Second Empire, 1860-1880 – The mansard roof is the most noteworthy feature of this style and is evidence of the French origins. Projecting central towers and one or two-story bays can also be present.

Vernacular/Traditional Mode 1638 - 1950
Influenced but not defined by a particular style, vernacular buildings are made from easily available materials and exhibit local design characteristics.

Other Books by Barbara Raue

Coins of Gold
Arrows, Indians and Love
The Life and Times of Barbara
The Cromwell Family Book
Laura Secord Discovered
Daddy Where Are You?

Montana Series
Book 1: Montana Dream
Book 2: Life on the Montana Frontier
Book 3: Montana to Boston and Back
Book 4: Montana Sons Go to War
Book 5: Montana Sons Return from War

Donaldson Series
Book 1: Rite of Passage
Book 2: Rite of Marriage

Other books on Haldimand County:
Fisherville, Nanticoke and Selkirk Ontario in Colour Photos
Cayuga and York Ontario in Colour Photos
Dunnville Ontario Book 1 in Colour Photos
Hagersville Ontario in Colour Photos
Jarvis and Port Dover Ontario in Colour Photos

Barbara is The Authority on Saving Our History One Photo at a Time. She is pursuing her interest in photography and architecture by preserving a record through photos of old buildings from the 1800s and 1900s with their unique architecture. Enjoy the beautiful architecture in the comfort of your living room. Dream about what it was like in those by-gone days. Dream about what it was like to live in a mansion like one of those in this book.

Barbara Raue, a wife, mother and grandmother, is an avid reader and writer. She has researched and compiled several family histories. In 2010, Barbara published her book "Coins of Gold," which celebrates the courageous life of her mother, May Todd. Barbara's second book is a historical fiction "Arrows, Indians and Love" which takes place in Boonesborough, Kentucky during the time of Daniel Boone. In 2013, Barbara published *The Cromwell Family Book* in which she traces her ancestry generations back into Great Britain. Her second novel is called *Laura Secord Discovered,* in which the story of Laura's service during the War of 1812 is shared. Barbara's memoir is titled *Daddy Where Are You?* It tells of her life growing up without a father. Five novels in the Montana Series have been published, *Montana Dream, Life on the Montana Frontier, Montana to Boston and Back, Montana Sons Go to War,* and *Montana Sons Return from War.* The Donaldson series of two novels is available: *Rite of Passage* and *Rite of Marriage.*

This is a link to Barbara's website to view all of her books
http://barbararaue.ca

www.ingramcontent.com/pod-product-compliance
Lightning Source LLC
Chambersburg PA
CBHW040230220526
45473CB00001B/185